WELCOME

to the Halal Keto Cookbook

TABLE OF CONTENTS

DEAR READERS,

In this book, I'm excited to share my personal collection of keto and low carb recipes that have brought joy to my culinary journey. While I'm not a professional dietitian or nutritionist, I am someone who simply loves food and has embraced the keto lifestyle. Like many of you, I struggled to find a diet that suited my needs and kept me motivated. However, everything changed when I was diagnosed with Hashimoto's disease, leading me to explore a specific dietary approach. But I didn't want to compromise on taste and enjoyment.

That's why I embarked on a mission to create a collection of keto recipes that not only follow the principles of the ketogenic diet but also deliver mouthwatering flavors and variety. These recipes have been carefully curated and tested in my own kitchen to ensure they're not only keto-friendly but also delicious.

I believe that eating healthy shouldn't be boring or tasteless. It should be an exciting journey of discovering new flavors, experimenting with ingredients, and savoring the pleasures of food. And as a devout Muslim, I understand the importance of aligning recipes with our cultural and religious beliefs.

As someone who faced weight issues and health concerns, I found the transformative power of the ketogenic diet. Through commitment and perseverance, I successfully shed 25 kilos and revitalized my overall well-being. But it wasn't just about aesthetics; it was also about addressing my specific health concerns.

Living with Hashimoto's disease and joint problems had taken a toll on my daily life. However, adopting the keto lifestyle brought remarkable improvements. I not only lost weight but also found relief from the symptoms associated with my conditions. Even my ovarian cysts gradually disappeared.

Additionally, I was thrilled to witness the positive effects of the keto diet on my skin. As a 44-year-old woman, I had battled with skin concerns, but the keto lifestyle brought about remarkable changes, such as improved tone and reduced appearance of wrinkles.

I'm excited to share these recipes with you, so you too can experience the benefits of a delicious and healthy keto lifestyle. Get ready to indulge in flavorful dishes that nourish your body and delight your taste buds.

Embark on this culinary journey with me and embrace the transformative power of the keto and low carb lifestyle. Let's make healthy eating an enjoyable and satisfying experience.

My skin transformed with a newfound radiance. The halal keto recipes I embraced nourished my skin from within, giving it a natural glow. Healthy fats and antioxidants in these recipes played a vital role in promoting cell regeneration and improving overall skin health.

Wrinkles gradually faded away as I adopted a low-carb, high-fat diet and increased collagen-rich foods. Collagen-boosting ingredients like bone broth, fish, and certain vegetables reduced the appearance of fine lines and wrinkles, leaving my skin supple and plump.

Sleep quality improved significantly. Insomnia and restless nights became a thing of the past, as deep, restorative sleep became the norm. Better sleep contributed to overall well-being and enhanced the health and vitality of my skin.

Mental clarity and focus soared with the keto diet. I experienced increased energy and productivity, bidding farewell to concentration problems and mental fog. Healthy fats and ketones as an energy source allowed my brain to function optimally, igniting enthusiasm and vigor in all aspects of life.

The halal keto lifestyle is a holistic approach to well-being. It promotes weight loss, addresses health concerns, and has a profound impact on our skin. By nourishing our bodies with wholesome, halal ingredients and embracing the ketogenic principles, we unlock a multitude of benefits, including radiant skin.

Inside this book, you'll find a wide range of keto recipes, from breakfasts to desserts. Detailed instructions and ingredient lists are provided, along with macronutrient information. Remember to consult a healthcare professional or dietitian for specific dietary concerns or medical conditions.

Embark on a culinary adventure, exploring vibrant flavors from Asia, aromatic spices from the Middle East, comforting classics from Europe, and bold dishes from the Americas. Experience the beauty of halal keto and embrace a healthier, more radiant you.

Whether you're a seasoned chef or a kitchen novice, this cookbook is here to guide you. With clear instructions, helpful tips, and stunning photography, each recipe will make your taste buds dance with anticipation.

I'm excited to share my passion for halal cooking and the incredible benefits of the ketogenic diet with you. This book is a valuable resource for Muslims seeking a healthier lifestyle without compromising on taste or cultural authenticity. Together, we can nourish our bodies and souls by combining the principles of halal and keto.

Get ready for a culinary voyage that celebrates the beauty of halal cuisine and empowers you to achieve your health and weight loss goals. Let The Halal Keto Cookbook be your guide, inspiring and satisfying you with every delicious bite.

Whether you're new to keto or a seasoned enthusiast, join me in exploring the world of delicious and satisfying meals. This book serves as your guide, a source of inspiration, and a reminder that keto can be both flavorful and enjoyable.

Wishing you a culinary adventure filled with mouthwatering dishes and the satisfaction of nourishing your body.

Happy cooking!

Azra

INTRODUCTION TO THE KETO DIET:

Understanding the Basics for Everyone

KETO

The ketogenic diet, commonly known as the keto diet, has gained popularity in recent years for its potential health benefits and weight loss effects. In this introduction, we will explore the fundamental principles of the keto diet, how it works, and the important things to know before embarking on this dietary approach.

What is the Keto Diet? The keto diet is a low-carbohydrate, high-fat diet that aims to shift your body's primary fuel source from carbohydrates to fat. By significantly reducing your carbohydrate intake and increasing your fat consumption, you enter a metabolic state called ketosis. In ketosis, your body becomes efficient at burning fat for energy, including stored body fat.

How Does the Keto Diet Work? The keto diet works by drastically reducing your carbohydrate intake, typically to around 20-50 grams per day, and increasing your fat intake to replace those calories. By restricting carbohydrates, your body depletes its glycogen stores, prompting the liver to produce ketones from fat. These ketones serve as an alternative fuel source for your body and brain.

Important Things to Know About the Keto Diet:

1. Macronutrient Ratio: The keto diet generally involves consuming 70-75% of your calories from fat, 20-25% from protein, and 5-10% from carbohydrates. This macronutrient ratio may vary slightly depending on individual needs and preferences.

2. Focus on Healthy Fats: While the keto diet emphasizes high fat intake, it's essential to choose healthy sources of fat. Opt for foods like avocados, nuts and seeds, olive oil, coconut oil, and fatty fish, which provide beneficial fats and important nutrients.

3. Carb Restriction: Carbohydrate restriction is a key aspect of the keto diet. Minimize your intake of high-carb foods such as grains, legumes, starchy vegetables, and most fruits. Instead, focus on low-carb options like leafy greens, non-starchy vegetables, and berries.

4. Adequate Protein Intake: Protein plays a vital role in the keto diet to support muscle maintenance and repair. Include moderate amounts of protein-rich foods such as lean meats, poultry, fish, eggs, and dairy products. Be mindful not to exceed your protein needs as excess protein can potentially affect ketosis.

5. Transition Period: When starting the keto diet, your body needs time to adapt to burning fat for fuel. This transition period, known as the "keto flu," may cause temporary symptoms like fatigue, headaches, and irritability. Stay hydrated, replenish electrolytes, and be patient as your body adjusts.

6. Importance of Nutrient Density: While following the keto diet, it's crucial to prioritize nutrient-dense foods to ensure you're getting essential vitamins, minerals, and fiber. Include a variety of vegetables, nuts, seeds, and low-carb fruits to meet your nutritional needs.

- Individualization and Monitoring: The keto diet may not be suitable for everyone, and it's important to listen to your body. If you have underlying health conditions or are taking medication, consult with a healthcare professional before starting the keto diet. Regular monitoring and adjustments may be necessary to ensure optimal results.
- Conclusion: The keto diet is a low-carbohydrate, high-fat dietary approach that aims to shift your body into a state of ketosis, where it burns fat for fuel. By understanding the principles and important considerations of the keto diet, you can make informed decisions about whether it aligns with your goals and individual needs. Remember, sustainable and balanced nutrition is key to any dietary approach, so always prioritize your overall health and well-being.

List of common ingredients and their corresponding keto alternatives. It can help you to turn your favorite recipes into keto.

1. Rice: Cauliflower rice, broccoli rice, or shirataki rice.
2. Sugar: Stevia, erythritol, monk fruit sweetener, or sugar alcohols.
3. Potato: Cauliflower, turnips, radishes, or celery root (celeriac).
4. Noodles: Zucchini noodles (zoodles), spaghetti squash, shirataki noodles, or kelp noodles.
5. Tortillas: Lettuce wraps, collard green wraps, or cheese wraps made from melted grated cheese.
6. Bread: Keto bread made with almond flour, coconut flour, or flaxseed meal.
7. Pasta: Zucchini noodles, spaghetti squash, shirataki noodles, or hearts of palm pasta.
8. Flour: Almond flour, coconut flour, flaxseed meal, or psyllium husk powder.
9. Milk: Unsweetened almond milk, coconut milk, or cashew milk.
10. Yogurt: Unsweetened Greek yogurt or coconut milk yogurt.
11. Oats: Ground flaxseed, chia seeds, or hemp hearts.
12. Breadcrumbs: almond flour, or ground flaxseed. Or ground the dried keto breads.
13. Sour Cream: Full-fat Greek yogurt or coconut cream.
14. Mayonnaise: Homemade keto-friendly mayonnaise or avocado oil-based mayo.
15. Cheese: Full-fat cheese varieties such as cheddar, mozzarella, or goat cheese.
16. Oil: Coconut oil, avocado oil, olive oil, or ghee (clarified butter).
17. Soy Sauce: Coconut aminos or tamari sauce (gluten-free soy sauce).
18. Cornstarch: Xanthan gum, guar gum, or arrowroot powder.
19. Peanut Butter: Almond butter, cashew butter, or sunflower seed butter.
20. Ice Cream: Sugar-free and low-carb ice cream made with natural sweeteners like stevia or erythritol.
21. Cereal: Homemade keto granola, crushed nuts, or coconut flakes.
22. Chocolate: Dark chocolate with a high percentage of cocoa (85% or more) or sugar-free chocolate.
23. Honey: Sugar-free honey substitutes like stevia or monk fruit syrup.
24. Ketchup: Sugar-free ketchup or homemade keto-friendly tomato sauce.
25. BBQ Sauce: Sugar-free BBQ sauce or homemade keto-friendly BBQ sauce

BREAKFAST RECIPES

KETO AVOCADO AND EGG SALAD

Directions

1 In a mixing bowl, combine the chopped hard-boiled eggs, diced avocados, mayonnaise, lemon juice, and chopped parsley.

2 Gently mash the avocados with a fork while mixing, until desired consistency is reached. Some prefer a chunkier texture, while others prefer it smoother.

3 Season the mixture with salt and pepper to taste, and mix well to incorporate all the ingredients.

4 Taste and adjust the seasoning or lemon juice if desired.

5 Serve the Keto Avocado and Egg Salad chilled, either as a side dish or on top of lettuce leaves for a refreshing salad option.

Ingredients

4 hard-boiled eggs, peeled and chopped

2 ripe avocados, pitted and diced

2 tablespoons mayonnaise

1 tablespoon lemon juice

2 tablespoons chopped fresh parsley

Salt and pepper to taste

KETO
MUSHROOM
OMLETTE

Ingredients

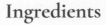

3 large eggs

240 g sliced mushrooms

240 g fresh spinach leaves

15 g butter or oil for cooking

Salt and pepper to taste

Optional: shredded cheese
(such as cheddar or
mozzarella) for topping

Directions

1 In a bowl, whisk the eggs until well beaten. Season with salt and pepper. Heat the butter or oil in a non-stick skillet over medium heat.

2 Add the sliced mushrooms to the skillet and sauté until they are tender and lightly browned, usually around 5 minutes.

3 Add the fresh spinach leaves to the skillet and cook until they are wilted, usually around 2 minutes. Reduce the heat to low and pour the beaten eggs over the mushrooms and spinach in the skillet. Tilt the skillet to ensure even distribution of the eggs.

4 Allow the omelette to cook undisturbed for a few minutes until the bottom sets. Carefully flip one half of the omelette over the other half, creating a half-moon shape.

5 Cook for an additional minute or two to ensure the eggs are fully cooked. If desired, sprinkle shredded cheese over the omelette and let it melt.

SMOKED SALMON AND CREAM CHEESE ROLL-UPS

Ingredients

115 grams smoked salmon

30 grams cream cheese

Fresh dill (optional)

Directions

1   Lay the smoked salmon slices on a flat surface.

2   Spread a thin layer of cream cheese on each slice.

3   Roll up the salmon slices and garnish with fresh dill, if desired.

KETO TURKISH BREAKFAST

Directions

1 Place the boiled/fried eggs in a bowl and sprinkle them with salt and pepper.

2 Heat a non-stick skillet over medium heat. Cook the sujuk slices until they are heated through and slightly crispy.

3 Arrange the boiled eggs, sujuk slices, feta cheese, olives, avocado, tomato, and cucumber on a plate.

4 Drizzle the olive oil over the ingredients and season with salt and pepper.

5 Garnish with fresh parsley.

Ingredients

4 boiled or fried eggs

4 pcs of Turkish sujuk (spicy beef sausage)

120 grams feta cheese, crumbled

120 grams olives (green or black)

1/2 avocado, sliced

1/2 medium-sized tomato, sliced

1/2 medium-sized cucumber, sliced

30 ml olive oil

Salt and pepper to taste

Fresh parsley for garnish

PERSIAN HERB OMLETTE

Directions

1 Preheat the oven to 175°C.
In a large mixing bowl, whisk the eggs until well beaten.

2 Add the chopped parsley, cilantro, dill, mint, green onions, and walnuts (if using) to the eggs. Mix well to combine.
Stir in the turmeric, baking powder, salt, and pepper. Make sure all the ingredients are evenly incorporated.

3 Heat the olive oil in an oven-safe non-stick skillet over medium heat.
Pour the egg mixture into the skillet and spread it out evenly.

4 Cook the omelette for about 5-7 minutes on the stovetop until the edges are set and the bottom is lightly golden.
Transfer the skillet to the preheated oven and bake for 10-12 minutes, or until the center is fully set and the top is lightly golden.

5 Remove the skillet from the oven and let the omelette cool for a few minutes.
Carefully slide a spatula around the edges of the omelette to loosen it from the skillet. Transfer it to a cutting board or serving plate.
Slice the omelette into wedges and serve warm.

Ingredients

4 large eggs

240 ml fresh parsley, finely chopped

240 ml fresh cilantro, finely chopped

240 ml fresh dill, finely chopped

120 ml fresh mint, finely chopped

2 green onions, finely chopped

60 g chopped walnuts

1/4 teaspoon turmeric

1/4 teaspoon baking powder

Salt and pepper to taste

15 ml olive oil

KETO EGG MUFFINS

Ingredients

6 large eggs

60 ml heavy cream

60 grams shredded cheddar
cheese

30 grams chopped spinach

Salt and pepper to taste

Directions

1   Preheat the oven to 190°C.

2   In a mixing bowl, whisk together the
eggs, heavy cream, salt, and pepper.
Stir in the shredded cheese and chopped
spinach.

3   Pour the mixture into a greased muffin
tin, filling each cup about three-quarters
full.

4   Bake for 20-25 minutes until the muffins
are set and slightly golden.

5   Allow them to cool before removing
from the tin.
Serve warm or refrigerate for later.

KETO CHIA PUDDING

Ingredients

30 grams chia seeds

120 ml unsweetened almond milk

1/4 teaspoon vanilla extract

Sweetener of choice (e.g., stevia, erythritol) to taste

Toppings: sliced almonds, berries, unsweetened coconut flakes (optional)

Directions

1 In a bowl or jar, combine the chia seeds, almond milk, vanilla extract, and sweetener.

2 Stir well.

3 Let the mixture sit for 5 minutes, then stir again to prevent clumping.

4 Cover and refrigerate overnight or for at least 2 hours until the chia seeds have absorbed the liquid and the mixture has thickened.

5 Serve chilled with your choice of toppings, such as sliced almonds, berries, or unsweetened coconut flakes.

KETO LÁNGOS

(HUNGARIAN FRIED DOUGH)

Directions

1 Separate the eggs, beat the egg whites, and mix the egg yolks with the cottage cheese, spices, and baking powder.

2 Then carefully add the beaten egg whites.

3 Step 2: Spread small heaps of the mixture onto a baking tray lined with parchment paper. Bake for 15 minutes.

4 Step 3: Once ready, remove from the parchment paper and sprinkle with garlic, sour cream, and cheese according to your taste.

Ingredients

250 g cottage cheese

6 g baking powder

4 eggs

A pinch of salt

1 teaspoon garlic powder

Toppings:

Garlic to taste

Sour cream to taste

Cheese to taste

MEDITERRANEAN

BAKED EGGS

Directions

1 Preheat the oven to 190°C.

2 In an oven-safe dish, combine the diced tomatoes, Kalamata olives, parsley, dried oregano, crushed red pepper flakes, salt, and pepper.

3 Make two wells in the tomato mixture and crack an egg into each well.

4 Bake in the preheated oven for about 10-12 minutes or until the eggs are cooked to your desired doneness. Serve hot.

Ingredients

4 large eggs

120g diced tomatoes

4 tablespoons chopped Kalamata olives

2 tablespoon chopped fresh parsley

1 teaspoon dried oregano

1/2 teaspoon crushed red pepper flakes

Salt and pepper to taste

KETO COCONUT FLOUR PANCAKES

Ingredients

2 tablespoons coconut flour

2 large eggs

1 tablespoon unsweetened almond milk

1/4 teaspoon baking powder

Sweetener of choice (e.g., stevia, erythritol) to taste

Butter or coconut oil for cooking

Directions

1 In a bowl, whisk together the coconut flour, eggs, almond milk, baking powder, and sweetener until well combined.

2 Heat butter or coconut oil in a non-stick skillet over medium heat.

3 Spoon the pancake batter onto the skillet, forming small pancakes.

4 Cook for 2-3 minutes on each side until golden brown.

5 Serve the pancakes with your choice of toppings, such as sugar-free syrup or berries.

KETO MANAKEESH ZAATAR

Ingredients

For the dough:

180 grams almond flour

20 grams ground flaxseed

5 grams baking powder

5 grams psyllium husk

powder

2.5 grams salt

15 ml olive oil

80 ml warm water

For the topping:

30 grams zaatar spice

30 ml olive oil

Directions

1 Preheat your oven to 200°C.

2 In a mixing bowl, combine the almond flour, ground flaxseed, baking powder, psyllium husk powder, and salt. Add the olive oil and warm water to the dry ingredients. Mix well until a dough forms.

3 Knead the dough for a few minutes until it becomes smooth and pliable. Divide the dough into smaller portions, depending on the size of the manakeesh you desire.

4 Place a portion of the dough between two sheets of parchment paper and roll it out into a round or oval shape, about ¼-inch thick.

5 Remove the top parchment paper and transfer the rolled dough onto a baking sheet.

6   Remove the top parchment paper and transfer the rolled dough onto a baking sheet.

7   In a small bowl, mix the zaatar spice and olive oil together to create a paste. Spread the zaatar paste evenly over the rolled dough.

8   Repeat the process for the remaining portions of dough.

9   Bake in the preheated oven for 10-12 minutes or until the edges of the manakeesh are golden brown.

10   Remove from the oven and let them cool for a few minutes.

11   Cut the manakeesh into wedges or squares and serve warm.

TURKISH

MENEMEN

Directions

1 Heat olive oil in a skillet over medium heat.

2 Add the thinly sliced onions and sauté until translucent. Stir in the sliced bell peppers and cook until they soften slightly.

3 Add the diced tomatoes, paprika, salt, and pepper. Cook for about 5 minutes until the tomatoes release their juices and create a sauce.

4 Create two small wells in the sauce and crack an egg into each well. Cover the skillet and cook for about 5-7 minutes or until the eggs are cooked to your desired doneness.

5 Garnish with fresh parsley and serve hot.

Ingredients

2 large eggs

1/2 medium onion, thinly sliced

1/2 medium green bell pepper, thinly sliced

1/2 medium red bell pepper, thinly sliced

2 medium tomatoes, diced

2 tablespoons olive oil

1/2 teaspoon paprika

Salt and pepper to taste

Fresh parsley for garnish

SHAKSHUKA

Directions

1 Heat olive oil in a skillet over medium heat.

2 Add the diced onions and bell peppers and cook until softened. Stir in the minced garlic, ground cumin, paprika, salt, and pepper.

3 Cook for another minute. Add the diced tomatoes and simmer for about 5 minutes until the sauce thickens slightly.

4 Create two small wells in the sauce and crack an egg into each well. Cover the skillet and cook for about 5-7 minutes or until the eggs are cooked to your desired doneness.

5 Garnish with fresh parsley and serve hot.

Ingredients

4 large eggs

160 g canned diced tomatoes

80 g diced bell peppers

80 g diced onions

1 clove garlic, minced

25 ml olive oil

1 teaspoon ground cumin

1 teaspoon paprika

Salt and pepper to taste

Fresh parsley for garnish

KETO GREEN SMOOTHIE

Directions

1 In a blender, combine all the ingredients and blend until smooth.

2 Add sweetener if desired and adjust the consistency with ice cubes if desired.

3 Pour into a glass and serve chilled.

Ingredients

1 cup unsweetened almond milk

1/2 ripe avocado

1 cup spinach

1/2 cucumber, peeled and chopped

1/4 cup fresh mint leaves

Juice of 1/2 lemon

Sweetener of choice (optional)

Ice cubes (optional)

BUJURDI – GREEK TOMATO-FETA BAKE

Ingredients

2 large tomatoes, sliced

1 large onion, sliced

2 bell peppers, sliced

200 grams of feta cheese,
crumbled

2 tablespoons of olive oil

Salt and pepper to taste

Fresh herbs for garnish

(optional)

Directions

1 Preheat your oven to 180°C .

2 In a large baking dish, arrange the tomato slices, onion slices, and bell pepper slices in layers.

3 Sprinkle crumbled feta cheese over the vegetables.

4 Drizzle olive oil evenly over the dish. Season with salt and pepper to taste. Bake in the preheated oven for about 25-30 minutes, or until the vegetables are tender and the cheese is golden and bubbly.

5 Remove from the oven and let it cool slightly.

6 Garnish with fresh herbs, such as parsley or cilantro, if desired.

CARDAMOM TOMATO BAKED EGG WITH CHEESE

Ingredients

1 ts Butter

Diced tomatoes

1 ts Tomato paste

Salt

Pepper

Ground cardamom

2 Boiled eggs (halved)

50 g Grated cheese (of your choice)

Directions

1 Heat a pan over medium heat and add butter.

2 Add diced tomatoes and tomato paste to the pan.

3 Season with salt, pepper, and ground cardamom.

4 Cook for approximately 10 minutes, allowing the flavors to meld and the sauce to thicken.

5 Add the halved boiled eggs to the pan. Sprinkle grated cheese on top of the mixture.

6 Cover the pan and let the cheese melt. Once the cheese has melted, remove from heat.

7 Serve the dish hot.

TURKISH EGG AND CHEESE

BOREK

Directions

1 Preheat the oven to 190°C.

2 Beat one egg in a bowl and set aside. Lay the phyllo sheet on a clean surface and brush it lightly with the beaten egg.

3 Sprinkle crumbled feta cheese and chopped parsley evenly over the phyllo sheet. Roll the phyllo sheet into a log and shape it into a spiral.

4 Transfer the spiral to a baking sheet lined with parchment paper. Brush the top with the remaining beaten egg.

5 Bake in the preheated oven for about 20-25 minutes or until golden brown. Allow it to cool slightly before serving.

Ingredients

2 large eggs

1 sheet of phyllo dough

60 g crumbled feta cheese

1 tablespoon chopped fresh parsley

Salt and pepper to taste

Olive oil or cooking spray

KETO BROCCOLI AND

CHEDDAR EGG MUFFINS

Directions

1 Preheat the oven to 175°C and grease a muffin tin.

2 In a bowl, whisk the eggs and season with salt and pepper.

3 Stir in the chopped broccoli and shredded cheddar cheese.

4 Pour the mixture into the greased muffin tin, filling each cup about 3/4 full.

5 Bake for 15-20 minutes or until the egg muffins are set and slightly golden.

Ingredients

6 large eggs

120 g chopped broccoli

60 g shredded cheddar cheese

Salt and pepper to taste

KETO GREEK YOGURT BOWL

Ingredients

120 ml Greek yogurt

60 g mixed berries (e.g.,

strawberries, blueberries,

raspberries)

1 tablespoon almond butter

1 tablespoon unsweetened

coconut flakes

Sweetener of choice

(optional)

Directions

1   In a bowl, layer the Greek yogurt, mixed berries, almond butter, and unsweetened coconut flakes.

2   Optional: Sweeten with your desired sweetener.

MEDITERRANEAN EGG SALAD

Ingredients

4 hard-boiled eggs, chopped

60 grams diced cucumber

60 grams diced tomatoes

60 grams diced red onion

4 tablespoons chopped

Kalamata olives

2 tablespoon chopped fresh

parsley

4 tablespoons extra virgin

olive oil

2 tablespoon lemon juice

Salt and pepper to taste

Directions

1   In a bowl, combine the chopped eggs, cucumber, tomatoes, red onion, Kalamata olives, and parsley.

2   In a separate small bowl, whisk together the olive oil, lemon juice, salt, and pepper.

3   Pour the dressing over the egg mixture and toss until well combined.

4   Adjust the seasoning if needed. Serve chilled.

KETO CAULIFLOWER

HASH BROWNS

Directions

1 In a bowl, combine the riced cauliflower, grated Parmesan cheese, egg, garlic powder, onion powder, salt, and pepper. Mix well.

2 Heat oil or butter in a non-stick skillet over medium heat.

3 Form the cauliflower mixture into small patties and place them on the skillet.

4 Cook for 3-4 minutes on each side until golden brown and crispy.

5 Remove from the skillet and serve hot.

Ingredients

400 g riced cauliflower

60 g grated Parmesan cheese

1 large egg

1/2 teaspoon garlic powder

1/2 teaspoon onion powder

Salt and pepper to taste

Cooking oil or butter for the pan

KETO GREEK FRITTATA

Directions

1 Preheat the oven to 175°C and grease a small baking dish.

2 In a bowl, whisk the eggs and season with salt and pepper.

3 Stir in the crumbled feta cheese, chopped Kalamata olives, diced tomatoes, and chopped fresh basil.

4 Pour the mixture into the greased baking dish and spread it evenly.

5 Bake for 15-20 minutes or until the frittata is set and slightly golden.

6 Allow it to cool for a few minutes before slicing and serving.

Ingredients

4 large eggs

60 g crumbled feta cheese

60 g chopped Kalamata olives

60 g diced tomatoes

2 tablespoons chopped fresh basil

Salt and pepper to taste

KETO ALMOND FLOUR PANCAKES

Ingredients

130 grams almond flour

35 grams coconut flour

4 large eggs

120 ml unsweetened almond milk

5 grams baking powder

Sweetener of choice (e.g., stevia, erythritol) to taste

Butter or coconut oil for cooking

Directions

1 In a bowl, whisk together the almond flour, coconut flour, eggs, almond milk, baking powder, and sweetener until well combined.

2 Heat butter or coconut oil in a non-stick skillet over medium heat.

3 Spoon the pancake batter onto the skillet, forming small pancakes.

4 Cook for 2-3 minutes on each side until golden brown.

5 Serve the pancakes with a drizzle of sugar-free syrup, if desired.

BAKED PROTEIN SHAKE

Ingredients

200ml natural yogurt

4 scoop of protein powder

2 eggs

Pinch of salt

Sweetener

Vanilla extract

1/2 tsp baking powder

For toppings : berries

(optional)

Directions

1 Start by preheating the oven to 180 degrees Celsius, ensuring that the convection setting is turned on.

2 Line a baking pan with baking paper. Combine the eggs, sweetener, vanilla extract, yogurt, and salt in a mixing bowl.

3 Next, incorporate the protein powder into the mixture.

4 Pour the batter into the prepared pan. Place the pan in the preheated oven and bake for approximately 25-30 minutes.

5 Decorate with Berries

KETO VEGETABLE BREAKFAST HASH

Ingredients

2 tablespoons olive oil

1/2 medium zucchini, diced

1/2 medium bell pepper, diced

1/4 medium onion, diced

60 g sliced mushrooms

2 eggs

Salt, pepper, and desired herbs/spices to taste

Directions

1 Heat olive oil in a skillet over medium heat.

2 Add the diced zucchini, bell pepper, onion, and sliced mushrooms.

3 Sauté until the vegetables are tender. Create two wells in the vegetable mixture and crack an egg into each well.

4 Season with salt, pepper, and desired herbs/spices.

5 Cover the skillet and cook until the eggs are cooked to your liking.
Serve hot.

BREAD ALTERNATIVES

pn

BREAD ALTERNATIVES AND IDEAS

When following a ketogenic diet, one of the biggest challenges is finding suitable alternatives for high-carb foods. One such food that many people miss on a keto diet is bread, which is typically high in carbohydrates. However, there are plenty of delicious and satisfying alternatives that can be used to create keto-friendly sandwiches. By replacing traditional bread with these alternatives, you can still enjoy your favorite sandwich fillings while staying in ketosis.

1. Lettuce Wrap Sandwich: Lettuce wraps are a popular choice for those on a keto diet. Crisp and refreshing lettuce leaves can be used as a replacement for bread, providing a low-carb and nutrient-rich base for your favorite fillings. Lettuce wraps are versatile and can be filled with various proteins, veggies, and condiments to create a satisfying and crunchy sandwich experience.

2. Portobello Mushroom Cap Sandwich: Portobello mushrooms offer a hearty and flavorful alternative to bread. Their large caps can be grilled or roasted to create a sturdy base for your sandwich fillings. The earthy taste of the mushrooms pairs well with a variety of ingredients, making it an excellent choice for a keto-friendly sandwich.

3. Collard Green Wrap: Collard greens are large, leafy greens that make excellent wraps. They have a slightly bitter taste that adds a unique flavor to your sandwich. Collard green wraps are sturdy and hold up well to fillings, providing a satisfying crunch. They are also packed with vitamins and minerals, making them a nutritious choice.

4. Cucumber Subs: Cucumbers can be sliced lengthwise and hollowed out to create a bread-like structure for your sandwich fillings. The crisp texture of cucumbers adds a refreshing element to your sandwich, while keeping the carb content extremely low. Cucumber subs are a great option for those looking for a light and hydrating alternative.

5. Egg Salad Lettuce Wraps: Egg salad is a classic sandwich filling, and you can enjoy it on a keto diet by using lettuce wraps instead of bread. Simply wrap your flavorful egg salad mixture in fresh lettuce leaves for a satisfying and protein-packed sandwich. It's a great way to enjoy the flavors of a traditional egg salad sandwich while keeping your carbs in check.

These keto sandwich alternatives provide a variety of options to satisfy your sandwich cravings while adhering to a low-carb, high-fat ketogenic diet. By choosing these alternatives, you can still enjoy the taste and satisfaction of a sandwich without compromising your nutritional goals. Experiment with different ingredients and combinations to find your favorite keto-friendly sandwich creations!

More ideas:
- Chicken Salad Stuffed Avocado
- Coconut Flour Wraps
- Keto Cheeseburger Lettuce Wraps
- Almond Flour Bread
- Zucchini Bun Sandwich
- Keto Pita Pocket
- Cauliflower Bread Sandwich
- Keto Tuna Salad Lettuce Wraps
- Bell Pepper Sandwiches
- Cloud Bread Sandwich
- Cheese tortilla wrap

KETO TORTILLA

(NO EGGS)

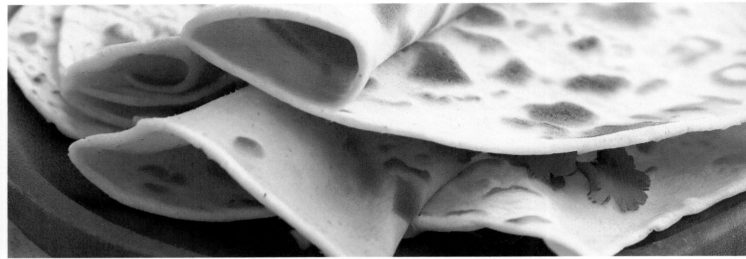

Directions

1. In a bowl, whisk together almond flour, coconut flour, baking powder, and salt.

2. Add olive oil and warm water to the dry ingredients and mix until a dough forms. Divide the dough into 4 equal portions and shape them into balls.

3. Place a dough ball between two sheets of parchment paper and roll it out into a thin circle.

4. Heat a non-stick skillet over medium heat and cook each tortilla for about 1-2 minutes on each side or until lightly browned. Repeat the process with the remaining dough balls.

5. Serve the keto tortillas warm or let them cool for later use.

Ingredients

250 g almond flour

2 tablespoons coconut flour

1/2 teaspoon baking powder

1/4 teaspoon salt

2 tablespoons olive oil

2 tablespoons warm water

EGG WRAPS

TORTILLA

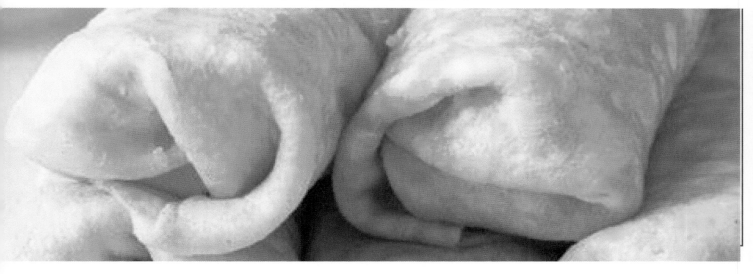

Directions

1 In a bowl, whisk together the eggs, salt, and pepper until well beaten.

2 Heat a non-stick skillet over medium heat and lightly grease it with cooking spray or oil.

3 Pour half of the egg mixture onto the skillet and quickly tilt the pan to spread the eggs into a thin, round shape.

4 Cook for about 1-2 minutes until set, then flip and cook for another 1-2 minutes.

Ingredients

2 large eggs ,

Pinch of salt

and pepper

COCONUT FLOUR TORTILLAS

Ingredients

60g coconut flour

6 eggs

300 ml unsweetened almond
milk

1/4 teaspoon baking powder

3/4 teaspoon of salt

Optional Add-ins
(Recommended):

1 tablespoon Unflavored
gelatin powder (for more
pliable, sturdy tortillas)

Directions

1 Whisk all ingredients in a large bowl until smooth. Let the batter sit for a minute to thicken.

2 Optional: Sprinkle gelatin over the batter, whisking to prevent clumping.

3 Heat a small skillet over medium-high heat and lightly grease with oil.

4 Pour 60ml of batter onto the skillet, tilting to distribute evenly.

5 Cook with a lid until edges turn golden and bubbles form in the middle (1-2 minutes).

6 Flip, cover, and cook for an additional 1-2 minutes until browned.

7 Repeat until all batter is used. Serve warm and use for desired dishes or fillings.

CHEESE TACO SHELLS

Ingredients

100 grams shredded

mozzarella cheese

25 grams grated Parmesan

cheese

1 large egg

Directions

1 In a microwave-safe bowl, combine the mozzarella cheese and Parmesan cheese. Microwave on high for 1 minute or until the cheeses are melted.

2 Stir the melted cheese mixture to ensure it's well combined.

3 Add the egg to the melted cheese mixture and mix until a dough forms.

4 Place the dough between two sheets of parchment paper and roll it out into a thin, round tortilla shape.

5 Heat a non-stick skillet over medium heat and cook the tortilla for about 1-2 minutes on each side until golden and crispy.

6 Remove the cooked cheese from the pan and place over a rolling pin (or something circular). Leave to cool. Remove and voila! A cheesy Taco Shell!

7 Fill with your choice of vegetables/meat/fish, eat and enjoy!

KETO WAFFLES

Directions

1   Preheat the waffle iron.

2   In a bowl, combine the dry ingredients: almond flour, coconut flour, psyllium husk powder, erythritol, baking powder, and salt. Set aside.

3   In a separate bowl mix the remaining ingredients: egg, cream cheese, butter, coconut oil, vanilla extract, and almond extract until well combined and smooth.

4   Add the dry ingredients to the wet mixture and continue mixing until you get a sticky batter.

5   Scoop the batter onto the preheated waffle iron. Cook until golden brown.

6   Serve the waffles with your favorite sugar- free toppings.

Ingredients

90 grams blanched almond flour

30 grams coconut flour

2 tablespoons psyllium husk powder

2 tablespoons keto sweetener

1 1/2 teaspoons baking powder

1/4 teaspoon salt

4 large eggs (room temperature)

60 grams block cream cheese,

40 grams butter

30 grams coconut oil

1 teaspoon vanilla extract

1/4 teaspoon almond extract

Topping : sugar-free maple syrup

KETO BREAD ROLLS

Directions

1 Preheat your oven to 175°C and line a baking sheet with parchment paper.

2 In a mixing bowl, whisk together the almond flour, psyllium husk powder, baking powder, and salt.
In a separate bowl, beat the eggs and then add the melted butter or coconut oil. Mix well.

3 Pour the wet ingredients into the dry ingredients and stir until combined. Gradually add the warm water while mixing, until a sticky dough forms.

4 Allow the dough to rest for a few minutes to allow the psyllium husk to absorb the moisture.
Divide the dough into six equal portions and shape each portion into a roll shape.

5 Place the rolls onto the prepared baking sheet and lightly flatten the tops.
Bake in the preheated oven for 35-40 minutes, or until the rolls are golden brown and firm to the touch.

Ingredients

180 grams almond flour

15 grams psyllium husk powder

5 grams baking powder

1/2 teaspoon salt

3 large eggs

60 grams melted butter or coconut oil

120 milliliters warm water

KETO NAAN BREAD

Ingredients

120 grams almond flour

15 grams coconut flour

15 grams psyllium husk
powder

5 grams baking powder

1/2 teaspoon salt

60 ml warm water

30 ml olive oil

30 ml plain Greek yogurt

1 large egg

Directions

1. In a bowl, mix together almond flour, coconut flour, psyllium husk powder, baking powder, and salt. In a separate bowl, whisk together warm water, olive oil, Greek yogurt, and egg.

2. Add the wet ingredients to the dry ingredients and mix until a dough forms. Divide the dough into 4 equal portions and shape them into balls.

3. Place a dough ball between two sheets of parchment paper and roll it out into a thin round shape.

4. Heat a non-stick skillet over medium heat and cook each naan bread for about 2-3 minutes on each side or until golden brown spots appear.

5. Repeat the process with the remaining dough balls. Serve the keto naan bread warm with melted butter, garlic and parsley.

KETO
BAGELS

Ingredients

240 grams almond flour

1 tablespoon baking powder

1/2 teaspoon salt

300 grams shredded

mozzarella cheese

60 grams cream cheese

2 large eggs

Bagel seasoning (optional)

mixture of sesame seeds,

poppy seeds, dried onion

flakes, dried garlic flakes, and

salt

Directions

1 Preheat your oven to 200°C and line a baking sheet with parchment paper.

2 In a microwave-safe bowl, combine the shredded mozzarella cheese and cream cheese. Microwave in 30-second intervals, stirring in between, until the cheeses are melted and well combined.

3 In a separate bowl, whisk together the almond flour, baking powder, and salt. Add the dry ingredients and eggs to the melted cheese mixture.

4 Mix well until a dough forms. Divide the dough into 6 equal portions. Roll each portion into a ball and use your finger to poke a hole in the center, shaping it into a bagel shape.

5 Place the bagels on the prepared baking sheet. If desired, sprinkle the tops with everything bagel seasoning. Bake in the preheated oven for 12-15 minutes, or until the bagels are golden brown.

KETO SLICED BREAD

Directions

1 Preheat the oven to 175°C. Grease a loaf pan and line it with parchment paper.

2 In a bowl, whisk together almond flour, ground flaxseed, coconut flour, baking powder, and salt.

3 In a separate bowl, whisk together eggs, melted butter, and almond milk.

4 Add the wet ingredients to the dry ingredients and mix until well combined. Pour the batter into the prepared loaf pan and smooth the top with a spatula.

5 Bake in the preheated oven for 40-45 minutes or until a toothpick inserted into the center comes out clean.

Ingredients

180 grams almond flour

35 grams ground flaxseed

15 grams coconut flour

1 teaspoon baking powder

1/2 teaspoon salt

4 large eggs

60 grams melted butter

60 ml unsweetened almond milk

CLOUD BREAD

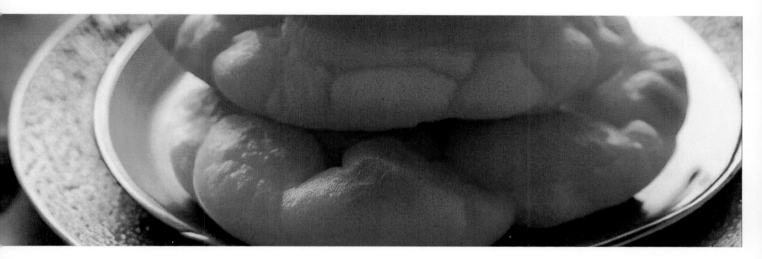

Directions

1 Preheat the oven to 150°C. Line a baking sheet with parchment paper.

2 In a bowl, beat the egg whites with cream of tartar until stiff peaks form. In another bowl, whisk together egg yolks, softened cream cheese, and salt until smooth. Gently fold the egg yolk mixture into the beaten egg whites until well combined.

3 Optional: Add herbs or spices for additional flavor and gently fold them into the mixture.

4 Spoon the mixture onto the prepared baking sheet, forming circles or desired shapes.

5 Bake in the preheated oven for about 25-30 minutes or until the cloud bread is golden brown and set. Allow the cloud bread to cool on a wire rack before serving.

Ingredients

3 large eggs, separated

3 tablespoons cream cheese, softened

1/4 teaspoon cream of tartar or baking pulver

1/4 teaspoon salt

Optional: herbs or spices for flavor (e.g., garlic powder, onion powder, dried herbs)

KETO ZUCCHINI BREAD

Ingredients

180 grams almond flour

30 grams coconut flour

1 teaspoon baking powder

1/2 teaspoon baking soda

1/2 teaspoon cinnamon

1/4 teaspoon salt

3 large eggs

60 ml melted coconut oil

60 ml unsweetened almond

milk

30 grams powdered erythritol

or low-carb sweetener of

choice

1 teaspoon vanilla extract

120 grams grated zucchini

Directions

1 Preheat the oven to 175°C. Grease a loaf pan and line it with parchment paper.

2 In a bowl, whisk together almond flour, coconut flour, baking powder, baking soda, cinnamon, and salt. In a separate bowl, whisk together eggs, melted coconut oil, almond milk, powdered erythritol, and vanilla extract.

3 Add the wet ingredients to the dry ingredients and mix until well combined. Fold in the grated zucchini until evenly distributed throughout the batter.

4 Pour the batter into the prepared loaf pan and smooth the top with a spatula.

5 Bake in the preheated oven for 45-50 minutes or until a toothpick inserted into the center comes out clean. Slice and serve when it cooled.

KETO ARABIC PITA BREAD

Ingredients

- 200 g shredded mozzarella cheese
- 25 g cream cheese
- 2 large eggs
- 200 g almond flour
- Salt to taste

Directions

1. Add the shredded mozzarella cheese and cream cheese to a microwave safe bowl and microwave on high in 30 second intervals. After every 30 seconds, stir the mixture until it's completely smooth.

2. Add the remaining ingredients. Add in the almond flour, eggs, and salt (to taste) and mix to combine.

3. Cover the dough mixture with plastic wrap and refrigerate for a minimum of one hour.

4. Preheat your oven to 180 C and prepare the dough for baking.
Divide the bread dough.

5. Line a baking sheet with parchment paper before dividing the bread dough into balls.

6. Place the balls evenly on the baking sheet. Bake the bread for 15-17 minutes.

HUNGARIAN CHEESE SCONE

Directions

1 Mix everything together in a bowl.

2 Preheat the oven to 180 Celcius. Put parchment paper in a pan.

3 Make balls from the dough with wet hands. Place them next to each other on the pan but leave a space between them.

4 Beat the eggs and wash the top with and sprinkle with cheese.

5 Bake for 25 minutes in the oven or until they are golden brown.

Ingredients

400g almond flour

1 tsp baking powder

1/2 tsp baking soda

1 tsp black pepper

2 tsp salt

2 eggs

250g butter

150g sour cream

150g grated cheese

For the Top:

1 egg

100g grated cheese

KETO GRISSINI

CRUNCHY KETO BREADSTICKS

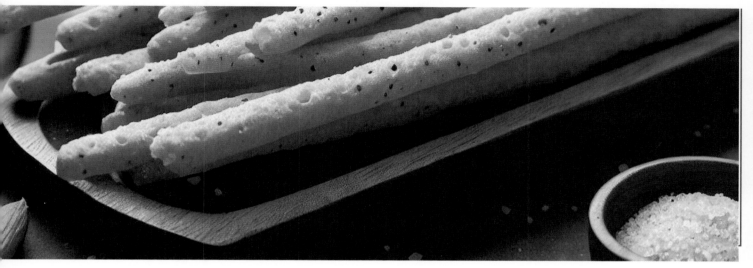

Directions

1 Mix the shredded cheese, cream cheese, garlic, rosemary, parsley, almond flour (or coconut flour) and a pinch of salt in a microwaveable bowl.

2 Microwave on high for 1 minute. Stir then microwave on high for another 30 seconds.

3 Add the egg then mix gently to make a cheesy dough.

4 Take small portions of the mozzarella dough and roll into a long, thin bread sticks. Place on a lined baking tray/sheet pan.

5 Bake at 220C for 10 minutes, or until golden brown. They may require more or less cooking time depending on how thin or thick you make your bread sticks.

Ingredients

170 grams grated mozzarella

85 grams almond flour

2 tablespoons Cream Cheese

Salt

1 Eggs

1 tablespoon Minced Garlic

1 teaspoon Dried Rosemary

1 tablespoon Parsley (fresh or dried)

KETO PIZZA CRUST

Ingredients

225 grams Shredded

Mozzarella Cheese

30 grams cream cheese

120 grams almond flour

1 large egg

4 grams baking powder (1

teaspoon)

2 grams Italian seasoning /

Oregano (optional)

Directions

1   Microwave the mozzarella and cream cheese for 45 seconds or until slightly melted.

2   Now stir until the cream cheese is fully incorporated. It may seem a little hard at first but will soon come together.

3   The next step is to simply add in the egg, almond flour, baking powder, and herbs. Mix until completely incorporated. The dough will seem sticky but that is fine.

4   To roll out the dough you have to options: because the dough is going to be soft and sticky, you can either roll it between two sheets of parchment paper or wet or grease your hands and pat it down flat with your hands.

5   The dough will need to be baked twice, once for the crust to bake and the next for the cheese and toppings. The first time it is baked for 10 minutes. While it's baking the first time, this would be a good time to prepare the toppings!

SALADS

KETO CHICKEN

CAESAR SALAD

Directions

1 Preheat your grill or stovetop grill pan over medium-high heat.

2 Rub the chicken breasts with olive oil, and season them with salt and pepper. Grill the chicken breasts for about 6-8 minutes per side, or until cooked through and no longer pink in the center. Remove from the grill and let them rest for a few minutes. Once cooled, slice the chicken into thin strips.

3 In a large salad bowl, combine the chopped romaine lettuce and grated Parmesan cheese. In a separate small bowl, whisk together the mayonnaise, grated Parmesan cheese, lemon juice, Dijon mustard, minced garlic, salt, and pepper to make the dressing.

4 Pour the dressing over the lettuce and toss until all the leaves are coated. Divide the salad into individual serving bowls or plates. Top the salad with the sliced grilled chicken. Optionally, garnish with additional Parmesan cheese and cracked black pepper.

Ingredients

2 boneless, skinless chicken breasts

2 tablespoons olive oil

Salt and pepper to taste

1 big romaine lettuce

30 grams grated Parmesan cheese

Ingredients for the Dressing:

60 grams mayonnaise

30 grams grated Parmesan cheese

1 tablespoon lemon juice

1 teaspoon Dijon mustard

1 clove garlic, minced

Salt and pepper to taste

KETO FATTOUSH SALAD

Directions

1 In a large salad bowl, combine the chopped romaine lettuce, diced cucumber, diced tomatoes, chopped parsley, and chopped mint.

2 In a separate small bowl, whisk together the extra virgin olive oil, lemon juice, minced garlic, sumac, salt, and pepper to make the dressing.

3 Pour the dressing over the salad and toss well to coat all the ingredients. Instead of the traditional arabic fried bread topping you can use melted cheese tortilla or other keto tortilla.

4 Make keto tortilla (Page 44), cut it for smaller pieces and roast in avocado oil to golden brown.

Ingredients

120 g chopped romaine lettuce

240 grams diced cucumber

240 grams diced tomatoes

120 grams chopped fresh parsley

60 grams chopped fresh mint

2tablespoons extra virgin olive oil

2 tablespoons lemon juice

1 clove garlic, minced

1 teaspoon sumac

Salt and pepper to taste

(Tortilla ingredients in page 44)

KETO TURKISH CUCUMBER YOGURT SALAD (CACIK)

Ingredients

1 medium cucumber, grated

230 g Greek yogurt

1 clove of garlic, minced

1 tablespoon fresh dill, chopped

1 tablespoon fresh mint, chopped

1 tablespoon lemon juice

Salt to taste

Directions

1   Place the grated cucumber in a sieve and squeeze out any excess liquid.

2   In a bowl, combine the cucumber, Greek yogurt, garlic, dill, mint, lemon juice, and salt. Mix well.

3   Refrigerate the salad for at least 30 minutes before serving to allow the flavors to meld together.

4   Serve chilled as a refreshing side dish or dip.

KETO TACO
SALAD

Ingredients

450 g ground beef

1 tablespoon taco seasoning

800g shredded lettuce

60g diced tomatoes

60g diced red onions

60g shredded cheddar cheese

60g sour cream

60g guacamole

Salsa for topping (optional)

Directions

1 In a skillet, cook the ground beef over medium heat until browned.

2 Drain excess fat.

3 Add taco seasoning and stir to coat the beef.

4 In a serving bowl, layer the shredded lettuce, seasoned ground beef, diced tomatoes, diced red onions, shredded cheddar cheese, sour cream, and guacamole.

5 Top with salsa if desired. Toss the salad before serving to combine the ingredients and enjoy!

BABA GANOUSH

Directions

1 Preheat the oven to 200°C.

2 Place the whole eggplants on a baking sheet and roast for 45-50 minutes until they are soft and collapsed.

3 Let the eggplants cool, then peel off the skin and discard it.

4 In a food processor or blender, combine the roasted eggplant flesh, minced garlic, tahini, lemon juice, olive oil, salt, and pepper. Blend until smooth and creamy.

5 Adjust the seasonings to taste. Serve the baba ganoush with cucumber or tomato slices or keto-friendly crackers. You can also make tortilla from mozzarella cheese in a pan.

Ingredients

2 medium-sized eggplants

2 cloves of garlic, minced

2 tablespoons tahini

2 tablespoons lemon juice

1 tablespoon olive oil

Salt and pepper to taste

KETO AVOCADO

CHICKEN SALAD

Directions

1 In a mixing bowl, mash the ripe avocado with a fork until smooth.

2 Add the shredded chicken, mayonnaise, lime juice, chopped fresh cilantro, diced red onions, salt, and pepper.

3 Mix well to combine all the ingredients.

4 Adjust seasoning if needed.

5 Serve the avocado chicken salad on lettuce leaves, low-carb wraps, or enjoy it as a topping for a bed of greens.

Ingredients

340 g cooked chicken breast, shredded

1 ripe avocado, peeled and pitted

30 grams mayonnaise

15 ml lime juice

15 g chopped fresh cilantro

35 g diced red onions

Salt and pepper to taste

KETO GREEK SALAD WITH GRILLED CHICKEN

Ingredients

340 grams cooked chicken breast, diced

75 grams diced cucumbers

35 grams diced red onions

35 g sliced Kalamata olives

35 g crumbled feta cheese

30 ml extra-virgin olive oil

15 ml fresh lemon juice

5 grams dried oregano

Salt and pepper to taste

Fresh parsley, for garnish

Directions

1. In a large mixing bowl, combine the diced chicken breast, cucumbers, red onions, Kalamata olives, and crumbled feta cheese.

2. In a small bowl, whisk together the olive oil, lemon juice, dried oregano, salt, and pepper.

3. Pour the dressing over the salad ingredients and toss well to coat.

4. Garnish with fresh parsley before serving.

GRILLED KETO HALLOUMI SALAD

Ingredients

110 g halloumi cheese

7-8 leaves of lettuce

45 g raspberries

20 g pumpkin seeds

1 small handful of parsley

1 tbsp extra virgin olive oil

1/2 tbsp balsamic vinegar

a pinch of black pepper

a pinch of salt (optional)

Directions

1   Slice the halloumi into thick slices.

2   Preheat a pan and grill the halloumi for a few minutes on each side until it turns golden brown.

3   Let the cheese cool down before adding it to the salad.

4   Toast the pumpkin seeds either in the oven or in a pan for a few minutes. Keep a close eye on them as they can burn quickly. Allow the seeds to cool down before adding them to the salad.

5   In a bowl, combine the chopped salad leaves with all the other ingredients. Just before serving, drizzle olive oil and balsamic vinegar over the salad.

KETO BIG MAC SALAD

Directions

1 In a medium skillet brown ground beef, then drain off any excess fat.

2 Add sugar-free ketchup, mustard, ketchup, mustard, Braggs aminos, Worcestershire, salt, pepper, and oregano.

3 Simmer on low for 2 minutes.

4 While it is simmering, wash and dry your lettuce, then chop and place it into four bowls.

5 Add the meat mixture, chopped onions, pickles, and tomatoes to each bowl.

6 Add the sauce ingredients to a small bowl then stir. Top each bowl with sauce and enjoy!

Ingredients

450 grams ground beef

2.5 -2.5 grams sugar-free ketchup, mustard , Worcestershire sauce

salt, pepper, soya sauce, oregano to taste

800 grams romaine lettuce, chopped

60 grams purple onion, chopped

80 grams grape tomatoes, quartered

140 grams shredded cheddar cheese

120 grams pickles, chopped

Big Mac Sauce:

118 grams mayo

30 grams chopped dill pickles

30 grams sugar-free ketchup

10 grams yellow mustard

5 grams vinegar

2.5 -2.5 grams paprika, garlic and onion powder

sweetener

THAI CHICKEN SALAD

Directions

1 Place all salad fixings in a large bowl, ensuring it is big enough for tossing. Set aside.

2 Make Dressing: In a medium microwave-safe bowl or measuring glass, combine all peanut dressing ingredients except for sesame oil.

3 Microwave the mixture uncovered until the peanut butter is just softened, for approximately 15 seconds at high power .

4 Whisk in the sesame oil until the dressing is very smooth and fully combined, which should take about a minute.

5 Toss Salad: Pour the peanut dressing over the salad fixings and toss the salad until it is well-mixed.

Ingredients

220 grams raw coleslaw mix

340 grams shredded cooked chicken

70 grams scallions, thinly sliced

120 g red bell pepper, thinly sliced

14 grams jalapeño, thinly sliced

60 grams roasted peanuts, roughly chopped

Peanut Dressing:

125 grams creamy peanut butter

60 grams toasted sesame oil

60 grams rice vinegar

60 grams water

15 grams sriracha

1 teaspoon salt

KETO TUNA LETTUCE WRAPS

Ingredients

150 g canned tuna (in brine or

olive oil, drained)

1 small ripe avocado

3-4 tbsp plain unsweetened

yogurt

10 green olives

2 tbsp extra virgin olive oil

juice of 1/2 lemon

1/2 tsp black mustard seeds,

crushed in a mortar

a pinch of black pepper

a pinch of salt

1/2 tsp freshly grated ginger

(optional)

8-10 leaves of lettuce

Directions

1   In a bowl, combine all the ingredients for the salad.

2   Use a fork to mash the avocado, ensuring a creamy consistency.

3   If needed, you can add more yogurt at the end and adjust the amount of spices according to your taste.

4   Fill the lettuce leaves with the prepared tuna salad.

5   Drizzle some olive oil over the top and sprinkle a pinch of black pepper for added flavor.

SOUPS

KETO BROCCOLI CHEDDAR SOUP

Ingredients

450 grams broccoli florets

2 tablespoons butter

70 grams small onion, diced

2 garlic cloves, minced

950 ml chicken or vegetable broth

240 grams heavy cream

225 grams shredded cheddar cheese

Salt and pepper to taste

Directions

1 In a large pot, melt the butter over medium heat. Add the diced onion and minced garlic, and sauté until the onion is translucent and fragrant.

2 Add the broccoli florets and cook for a few minutes until slightly tender. Pour in the chicken or vegetable broth and bring to a boil.

3 Reduce the heat and let it simmer for about 10-15 minutes until the broccoli is fully cooked. Use an immersion blender or transfer the mixture to a blender to puree the soup until smooth.

4 Return the soup to the pot over low heat and stir in the heavy cream and shredded cheddar cheese until melted and well combined.

5 Season with salt and pepper to taste. Continue to heat the soup until it's hot, but be careful not to let it boil. Serve hot and garnish with additional shredded cheddar cheese if desired.

KETO TOMATO BASIL SOUP

Ingredients

2 tablespoons olive oil

30g diced onion

2 cloves garlic, minced

500 g canned crushed
tomatoes

250 ml chicken or vegetable
broth

60 g heavy cream

1 teaspoon dried basil

Salt and pepper to taste

Fresh basil for garnish

Directions

1   Heat the olive oil in a pot over medium
     heat.

2   Add the diced onion and minced garlic.
     Sauté until the onions are translucent and
     the garlic is fragrant.

3   Add the crushed tomatoes and chicken or
     vegetable broth to the pot. Bring to a
     simmer.

4   Stir in the heavy cream and dried basil.
     Season with salt and pepper to taste.

5   Simmer for 10-15 minutes to allow the
     flavors to meld together.

6   Use an immersion blender or transfer the
     soup to a blender to puree until smooth.

7   Ladle the soup into bowls and garnish with
     fresh basil. Serve hot.

KETO GOULASH

(HUNGARIAN BEEF STEW)

Directions

1. In a large pot or Dutch oven, heat the olive oil over medium heat.

2. Add the diced onion and minced garlic to the pot and sauté until translucent.

3. Add the beef stew meat to the pot and brown it on all sides. Stir in the diced bell peppers, tomatoes, paprika, caraway seeds, salt, and black pepper.

4. Cook for a few minutes until the vegetables are slightly softened. Pour in the beef broth and bring the mixture to a boil.

5. Reduce the heat to low, cover the pot, and let it simmer for about 2 hours or until the beef is tender. If desired, garnish with a dollop of sour cream before serving. Note: The calorie count may vary depending on the specific cut of beef used and the serving size.

Ingredients

700 g beef stew meat, cut into bite-sized pieces

1 tablespoon olive oil

1 medium onion, diced

2 cloves garlic, minced

2 bell peppers, diced

2 medium tomatoes, diced

1 tablespoon paprika

1/2 teaspoon caraway seeds

1 teaspoon salt

1/2 teaspoon black pepper

2 cups beef broth

Sour cream (optional garnish)

KETO CAULIFLOWER SOUP

Directions

1 Preheat the oven to 200°C. Place the cauliflower florets on a baking sheet, drizzle with olive oil, and season with salt and pepper.

2 Roast for 20-25 minutes until the cauliflower is tender and slightly caramelized.

3 In a large pot, heat olive oil over medium heat. Add the diced onion and minced garlic. Sauté until the onions are translucent and the garlic is fragrant.

4 Add the roasted cauliflower and broth to the pot. Bring to a simmer and cook for 10 minutes. Use an immersion blender or transfer the soup to a blender to puree until smooth.

5 Return the soup to the pot and stir in the heavy cream and dried thyme. Season with salt and pepper to taste. Serve hot, garnished with chopped fresh parsley.

Ingredients

1 medium head cauliflower, cut into florets

2 tablespoons olive oil

30g diced onion

2 cloves garlic, minced

1000 ml vegetable or chicken broth

120g heavy cream

1 teaspoon dried thyme

Salt and pepper to taste

Chopped fresh parsley for garnish

KETO GARLIC CREAM SOUP WITH GOLDEN CHEESE CRISPS

Ingredients

4 tablespoons butter

6 cloves garlic, minced

1000ml chicken or vegetable

broth

120 g heavy cream

1/2 teaspoon dried thyme

Salt and pepper to taste

1 cup shredded cheddar

cheese

For the Golden Cheese

Crisps:

1 cup shredded mozzarella

cheese

Directions

1 Preheat the oven to 190°C.
In a large pot, melt the butter over medium heat. Add minced garlic and sauté until fragrant.

2 Pour in chicken or vegetable broth and bring to a simmer. Cook for about 10 minutes to infuse the garlic flavor.

3 Reduce the heat to low and stir in heavy cream and dried thyme. Simmer for an additional 5 minutes. Season the soup with salt and pepper to taste.

4 Line a baking sheet with parchment paper. Take small piles of shredded mozzarella cheese and spread them out on the prepared baking sheet, forming thin circles.

5 Bake the cheese crisps in the preheated oven for about 5-7 minutes, until golden brown and crispy. Remove from the oven and let them cool completely.

6 Once cooled, remove the cheese crisps from the baking sheet and set aside.
Garnish each bowl with a few golden cheese crisps on top.

KETO CELERY SOUP

Ingredients

150g Celery

100g Parsnip

1 Egg

Coconut Milk

350ml Water

15g Coconut Oil

Salt to taste

5g Tandoori Coconut Spice

Toppings: Roasted Pumpkin
or Carrot Slices

Directions

1 Cut the vegetables into small pieces.

2 Heat coconut oil and seasoning oil in a pot and roast the vegetables in it. The roasting aroma enhances the flavor of the soup!

3 After roasting the vegetables, add water and coconut milk to the pot and let it simmer with the lid on until the vegetables become soft.

4 Transfer everything to a blender and blend until smooth. Return the mixture to the pot.

5 If the soup is too thick, add some water until desired consistency is reached. Season the soup with sea salt.

6 Crack the egg into a glass. Gently stir the soup to create a swirl, then add the egg to the center. Cover and let it simmer gently to keep the egg intact.

7 Carefully pour the soup into a bowl. Garnish with Roasted Pumpkin seeds or Carrot Slices

HUNGARIAN TARRAGON

CHICKEN RAGOUT SOUP

Directions

1 Start melting the butter over medium heat while finely chopping the onions.

2 Once the onions are nicely sautéed, add the sliced zucchini and continue sautéing for another 5 minutes. After the zucchini, add the green beans and broccoli.

3 When the vegetables are slightly sautéed, add the chopped chicken breast.

4 Pour in the chicken or vegetable broth and season with tarragon (fresh or dried), salt, and pepper. Bring it to a boil and let it simmer for 5 minutes after reaching a boil.

5 Add the grated garlic. Once the soup has simmered enough, add the cream and continue boiling for another 5 minutes. Serve hot.

Ingredients

500g chicken breast

1/2 onion

1 zucchini

200g broccoli

200g green beans

2 tablespoons butter

3 dl (300ml) cream

1.5 liters chicken or vegetable broth

1 clove grated garlic

Tarragon to taste

Salt and pepper to taste

KETO SHRIMP CURRY

COCONUT MILK SOUP

Directions

1 Finely chop the ginger, shallot, garlic cloves, red bell pepper, and mushrooms.

2 Melt the butter in a pot over medium-high heat and add the ginger, shallot, and garlic. Sauté for 3-4 minutes.

3 Add the frozen shrimp to the pot and cook for about 6-7 minutes until they turn pink and are cooked through. Add the chopped red bell pepper and mushrooms to the pot and sauté for 5 minutes.

4 Prepare the vegetable broth according to the package instructions. Then, add the curry powder, salt, and pepper to the pot and stir briefly.

5 Pour in the vegetable broth and coconut milk, and let everything simmer for another 5-10 minutes. Remove the soup from the heat and squeeze in the lime juice. Serve with fresh cilantro, if desired.

750ml vegetable broth

400ml full-fat coconut milk

300g frozen shrimp

300g mushrooms

1 red bell pepper

1 shallot

2 garlic cloves

1 lime (juice)

15g ginger

1 tbsp butter

1 tbsp curry powder

1 tsp salt

1/4 tsp pepper

Optional: fresh cilantro

MAIN DISHES

Lunch or Dinner recipes

KETO SALMON WITH

LEMON DILL SAUCE

Directions

1 Preheat your oven to 375°F (190°C). Season the salmon fillets with salt and pepper on both sides.

2 In an oven-safe skillet or baking dish, heat the olive oil over medium-high heat. Place the seasoned salmon fillets in the skillet, skin side down. Sear the salmon for about 2-3 minutes until the skin is crispy and browned.

3 Transfer the skillet to the preheated oven and bake the salmon for about 10-12 minutes, or until it flakes easily with a fork and reaches your desired level of doneness.

4 While the salmon is baking, prepare the Lemon Dill Sauce by combining the mayonnaise, lemon juice, chopped dill, minced garlic, salt, and pepper in a small bowl. Stir well to combine.

5 Once the salmon is cooked, remove it from the oven and let it rest for a few minutes. Serve the salmon fillets with a generous dollop of the Lemon Dill Sauce on top. Garnish with additional fresh dill, if desired

Ingredients

2 salmon fillets

Salt and pepper to taste

2 tablespoons olive oil

For the Lemon Dill Sauce:

1/4 cup mayonnaise

2 tablespoons fresh lemon juice

1 tablespoon chopped fresh dill

1 clove garlic, minced

Salt and pepper to taste

KETO STEAK WITH GARLIC BUTTER

Ingredients

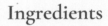

450 g steak (such as sirloin or ribeye), cut into bite-sized cubes

2 tablespoons butter

3 cloves garlic, minced

1 tablespoon chopped fresh parsley

Salt and pepper to taste

Directions

1 In a large skillet, melt the butter over medium-high heat.

2 Add the minced garlic and cook for 1-2 minutes until fragrant.

3 Add the steak bites to the skillet and cook for 2-3 minutes per side for medium-rare, or longer depending on your desired level of doneness.

4 Season with salt and pepper to taste.

5 Remove from heat and sprinkle with chopped fresh parsley. Let the steak bites rest for a few minutes before serving.

KETO CAULIFLOWER FRIED RICE

Ingredients

1 medium head cauliflower, riced

2 tablespoons sesame oil

2 cloves garlic, minced

1/2 cup diced carrots

1/2 cup diced bell peppers

1/4 cup diced green onions

2 eggs, beaten

2 tablespoons soy sauce (or tamari for gluten-free)

Salt and pepper to taste

Directions

1 Heat sesame oil in a large skillet or wok over medium heat.

2 Add minced garlic and sauté for 1-2 minutes until fragrant.

3 Add the riced cauliflower and cook for 5 minutes, stirring frequently.

4 Push the cauliflower to one side of the skillet and pour the beaten eggs into the other side.

5 Scramble the eggs until cooked, then combine with the cauliflower.

6 Add diced carrots, bell peppers, and green onions to the skillet and cook for an additional 5 minutes until the vegetables are tender.

7 Stir in soy sauce and season with salt and pepper. Serve hot.

KETO CHICKEN ALFREDO

CASSEROLE

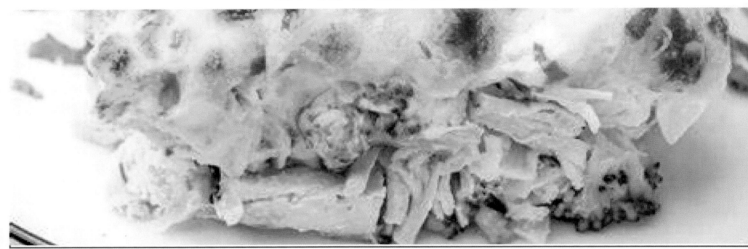

Directions

1 Preheat oven to 200°C.
Place the chicken and broccoli in a baking dish.

2 In a skillet, melt butter over medium heat.
Add onion and cook for 2-3 minutes.
Add garlic and cook for 30 seconds.

3 Stir in heavy cream and cream cheese, cooking for 3-4 minutes until the sauce thickens. Remove from heat. Mix in chopped parsley. Season with salt and black pepper to taste.

4 Pour the sauce over the chicken and broccoli.
Sprinkle grated Parmesan on top.

5 Bake in the preheated oven for 25-30 minutes until the broccoli is tender and the sauce is golden and bubbly. Garnish with extra parsley and serve.

Ingredients

2 boneless, skinless chicken breasts

Salt and pepper to taste

2 tablespoons olive oil

4 cloves garlic, minced

240 g heavy cream

90g grated Parmesan cheese

60g unsalted butter

1/2 teaspoon Italian seasoning

Fresh parsley, chopped (for garnish)

KETO EGGPLANT PARMESAN

Directions

1 Preheat oven to 190°C. Slice eggplant into 1 cm rounds, salt both sides, and let sit for 10-15 minutes.

2 Combine almond flour, Parmesan cheese, and Italian seasoning. Whisk eggs in a separate bowl.

3 Rinse and dry eggplant slices. Dip each slice in beaten eggs, then coat with almond flour mixture.

4 Cook coated slices in olive oil on medium heat for 2-3 minutes per side. Transfer cooked slices to paper towels.

5 Spread marinara sauce in baking dish.

6 Layer cooked eggplant slices, more sauce, and shredded mozzarella cheese.

7 Repeat layering. Bake for 20-25 minutes until cheese melts. Let cool briefly, garnish with basil leaves, and serve hot as a main dish or with a side salad.

Ingredients

1 large eggplant

Salt for sprinkling

1 cup almond flour

1/2 cup grated Parmesan cheese

2 teaspoons Italian seasoning

2 large eggs

2 tablespoons olive oil

1 cup low-carb marinara sauce

1 cup shredded mozzarella cheese

Fresh basil leaves for garnish

KETO MEATBALLS WITH MARINARA SAUCE

Ingredients

450 g ground beef

30g almond flour

30 g grated Parmesan cheese

30 g chopped fresh parsley

1 clove garlic, minced

1 egg

1 teaspoon dried oregano

1/2 teaspoon salt

1/4 teaspoon black pepper

450 g marinara sauce

Directions

1 Preheat the oven to 200°C.

2 In a large mixing bowl, combine ground beef, almond flour, grated Parmesan cheese, chopped fresh parsley, minced garlic, egg, dried oregano, salt, and black pepper.

3 Mix well using your hands until all ingredients are evenly incorporated. Shape the mixture into meatballs, approximately 2,5 cm in diameter.

4 Place the meatballs on a greased baking sheet and bake for 15-20 minutes until cooked through.

5 Heat the marinara sauce in a saucepan over medium heat.

6 Add the cooked meatballs to the sauce and simmer for 5 minutes to coat them evenly. Serve hot.

KETO CHEESEBURGER LETTUCE WRAPS

Ingredients

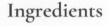

450 g ground beef

Salt, pepper oregano to taste

4 slices of cheddar cheese

4 large lettuce leaves (such as

iceberg or butter lettuce)

4 slices of tomato

4 slices of red onion

Pickles,Mustard,Ketchup,

Mayo optional

Directions

1 Preheat a grill or skillet over medium heat.

   In a large bowl, combine ground beef, seasoned salt, pepper, and oregano.

2 Shape the mixture into 6 equal-sized balls, then flatten each ball to form a patty.

3 Place the patties on the grill or skillet and cook for about 4 minutes on each side, or until they reach your desired level of doneness.

4 Place a slice of cheese on top of each cooked burger.

   Place each burger on a large lettuce leaf.

5 Top with the spread, a slice of tomato, red onion, and any additional toppings you prefer. Fold the lettuce leaf over the top of the burger and serve.

KETO CHICKEN

STIR-FRY

Directions

1 Season chicken breasts with salt and pepper.

2 In a skillet or wok, heat coconut oil over medium-high heat. Cook the chicken for 5-6 minutes until cooked through. Set aside.

3 In the same skillet, add garlic and ginger. Sauté for 1 minute.

4 Add broccoli, red bell pepper, zucchini, and mushrooms. Stir-fry for 4-5 minutes until crisp-tender.

5 Add chicken back to the skillet.

6 In a small bowl, whisk soy sauce, sesame oil, and rice vinegar. Pour over chicken and vegetables.

7 Stir-fry for 2-3 minutes. Remove from heat. Serve hot, optionally topped with sesame seeds and green onions.

Ingredients

2 boneless, skinless chicken breasts,

Salt and pepper to taste

2 tablespoons coconut oil

2 cloves garlic, minced

1 tablespoon grated ginger

1 cup broccoli florets

1 red bell pepper, sliced

1 small zucchini, sliced

1/2 cup sliced mushrooms

2 tablespoons low-sodium soy sauce

1 tablespoon sesame oil

1 tablespoon rice vinegar

Optional : sesame seeds, green onions

HUNGARIAN SAUERKRAUT

STEW (SZÉKELYKÁPOSZTA)

Directions

1 Start by sautéing 40g of turkey bacon or ham in the Instant Pot with olive oil. It is important because of the smokey taste.

2 Add chopped onions and mix well. Next, add the beef shoulder cubes and sausage to the pot. Season with salt and black pepper. Mix until the meat turns white.

3 Drain the water from the sauerkraut and add it to the instant pot. Mix well to incorporate the sauerkraut with the meat.

4 Add paprika powder and more salt to achieve a nice orange color. Add approximately 1 cup of water to the pot, depending on its size.

5 Close the lid, move the valve to "sealing," and set it to cook for 45 minutes under high pressure. Once done, press cancel and perform a quick release by moving the valve to "venting."

6 Mix everything well before serving. Serve the Székelykáposzta in bowls and add full-fat sour cream.

Ingredients

2000g Sauerkraut

800g beef shoulder cut in cubes

150g Spicy smokey halal sausage

40g turkey bacon or smoked ham

10ml olive oil

15g chopped onions

15g paprika powder

Salt to taste

Ground black pepper

Toppings: Some sour cream

KETO SHRIMP SCAMPI WITH ZUCCHINI NOODLES

Ingredients

2 medium zucchini -

450 g shrimp, peeled and
deveined

Salt and pepper to taste

3 tablespoons unsalted butter

3 cloves garlic, minced

1/4 teaspoon red pepper
flakes (optional)

60 ml chicken or vegetable
broth

2 tablespoons lemon juice -

2 tablespoons chopped fresh
parsley

Lemon wedges for serving

Directions

1   Using a spiralizer or vegetable peeler, make zoodles from the zucchini. Set aside.

2   Season shrimp with salt and pepper.

3   In a skillet, melt butter over medium heat. Add garlic and red pepper flakes (optional) to the skillet and sauté for 1 minute.

4   Add the seasoned shrimp to the skillet and cook for 2-3 minutes per side until pink and cooked through.

5   Remove cooked shrimp and set aside. In the same skillet, add broth and lemon juice. Simmer for 2 minutes.

6   Add zoodles to the skillet and toss to coat in the sauce. Cook for 2-3 minutes until tender.

7   Return cooked shrimp to the skillet and stir in parsley. Serve the Keto Shrimp Scampi with Zucchini Noodles hot, garnished with lemon wedges.

KETO TURKISH STUFFED BELL PEPPERS (BIBER DOLMASI)

Ingredients

4 medium bell peppers (any color)

225 g ground beef or lamb

1/4 cup cauliflower rice

1 small onion, finely chopped

2 cloves of garlic, minced

2 tablespoons tomato paste

2 tablespoons olive oil

1 teaspoon ground cumin

1 teaspoon ground paprika

Salt and pepper to taste

Fresh parsley for garnish

Directions

Preheat the oven to 350°F (175°C).

1 Cut off the tops of the bell peppers and remove the seeds and membranes. Set aside.

2 In a skillet, heat the olive oil over medium heat. Add the onion and garlic and sauté until softened.

3 Add the ground beef or lamb to the skillet and cook until browned. Drain any excess fat.

4

5 Stir in the cauliflower rice, tomato paste, cumin, paprika, salt, and pepper. Cook for an additional 2-3 minutes.

Stuff the bell peppers with the meat mixture and place them in a baking dish.

Cover the dish with foil and bake for 30-35 minutes, or until the bell peppers are tender. Remove the foil and bake for an additional 5-10 minutes to allow the tops to brown slightly.

KETO TURKISH LAMB KEBABS

Directions

1 In a bowl, combine the lamb cubes, onion, garlic, olive oil, cumin, paprika, salt, and pepper.

2 Mix well to ensure the meat is evenly coated with the spices.

3 Cover the bowl and marinate the lamb in the refrigerator for at least 1 hour.

4 Preheat the grill or grill pan over medium heat. Thread the marinated lamb cubes onto skewers.

5 Grill the kebabs for about 10-12 minutes, turning occasionally, until the lamb is cooked to your desired doneness.

6 Serve the kebabs with a side salad or steamed vegetables.

Ingredients

225 g lamb, cut into small cubes

1 small onion, finely chopped

2 cloves of garlic, minced

1 tablespoon olive oil

1 teaspoon ground cumin

1 teaspoon ground paprika

Salt and pepper to taste

KETO BAKED FISH IN A COAT

Directions

1 Preheat oven to 200°C. Prepare a baking sheet.

2 In a bowl, combine almond flour, grated Parmesan cheese, paprika, garlic powder, dried parsley, salt, and pepper.

3 Coat each fish fillet in melted butter or olive oil.

4 Dredge the coated fish fillets in the almond flour mixture.

5 Place the coated fish fillets on the baking sheet.

6 Bake for 15-20 minutes until fish is cooked and coating is golden and crispy. Let cool briefly before serving.

Ingredients

4 fish fillets (such as cod, haddock, or tilapia)

1/2 cup almond flour

1/4 cup grated Parmesan cheese

1 teaspoon paprika

1/2 teaspoon garlic powder

1/2 teaspoon dried parsley

Salt and pepper to taste

2 tablespoons melted butter or olive oil

KETO-FRIENDLY MAKLOUBA

Ingredients

1 medium-sized cauliflower

450 g boneless chicken thighs,
cut into bite-sized pieces

2 tablespoons olive oil

1 small eggplant, sliced into
rounds

1 small zucchini, sliced into
rounds

1 small head of cauliflower, cut
into florets

1 teaspoon ground cumin

1 teaspoon ground turmeric

1 teaspoon ground cinnamon

1/2 teaspoon ground black
pepper

1/2 teaspoon salt (or to taste)

1/4 cup chopped fresh parsley
(for garnish)

Directions

1   Preheat the oven to 400°F (200°C).

2   Prepare cauliflower rice by pulsing small florets in a food processor.

3   Brown the chicken in olive oil, then set aside.

4   Sauté the sliced eggplant and zucchini until slightly softened, then remove from pan.

5   Cook cauliflower rice and florets for 5 minutes.

6   Combine cooked chicken, sautéed vegetables, and cauliflower in the pan. Sprinkle with spices and stir to combine.

7   Transfer mixture to a baking dish and cover with foil. Bake for 25-30 minutes until cauliflower is tender. Let it rest before inverting onto a serving platter. Garnish with fresh parsley.

KETO ZUCCHINI LASAGNA

Ingredients

3 medium zucchini

450 g ground beef

1/2 small onion, diced

2 cloves garlic, minced

1 cup low-carb marinara sauce

1 teaspoon dried basil

1 teaspoon dried oregano

Salt and pepper to taste

240g ricotta cheese

120 g shredded mozzarella cheese

30 g grated Parmesan cheese

Fresh basil leaves for garnish

Directions

1 Preheat oven to 190°C.

2 Slice zucchini into thin strips. Sprinkle with salt, let sit to remove moisture, then pat dry.

3 Cook ground beef with onion and garlic. Add marinara sauce, basil, oregano, salt, and pepper.

4 In a separate bowl, mix ricotta, mozzarella, and Parmesan.

5 In a baking dish, layer meat sauce, zucchini, and cheese mixture. Repeat layers and finish with meat sauce on top.

6 Bake covered for 30 minutes, then uncovered for 10-15 minutes.
Garnish with basil leaves.

KETO GARLIC PARMESAN

WINGS

Directions

1 Preheat oven to 220°C. Line a baking sheet.

2 Pat dry chicken wings, place on baking sheet. Season with salt and pepper.

3 Bake for 40-45 minutes until crispy and cooked through. Flip halfway.

4 Prepare garlic Parmesan coating: mix grated Parmesan, minced garlic, melted butter, parsley, and optional red pepper flakes.

5 Remove wings from oven, transfer to bowl. Add coating, toss to coat.

6 Return wings to baking sheet, broil for 2-3 minutes until golden and crispy. Let cool. Serve hot, garnish with Parmesan and parsley.

Ingredients

900g chicken wings

Salt and pepper to taste

50g grated Parmesan cheese

2 tablespoons minced garlic

2 tablespoons melted butter

1 tablespoon chopped fresh parsley

Optional: red pepper flakes for a spicy kick

KETO COCONUT CURRY

CHICKEN

Directions

1 In a large skillet, heat the coconut oil over medium heat.

2 Add the diced onion, minced garlic, and grated ginger. Sauté for 2-3 minutes until fragrant.

3 Add the chicken pieces to the skillet and cook until browned on all sides.

4 Stir in the curry powder, coconut milk, and chicken broth. Bring to a simmer and cook for 10 minutes.

5 Add the diced bell peppers and broccoli florets, and continue to simmer for another 5-7 minutes until the vegetables are tender.

6 Season with salt and pepper to taste. Garnish with chopped fresh cilantro before serving. Serve over cauliflower rice or enjoy on its own.

Ingredients

450 grams chicken breasts, cut into bite-sized pieces

15 grams coconut oil

1 small onion, diced

2 cloves garlic, minced

15 grams grated fresh ginger

15 grams curry powder

1 can (400 ml) coconut milk

240 ml chicken broth

120 grams diced bell peppers

120 grams broccoli florets

Salt and pepper to taste

Chopped fresh cilantro, for garnish

KETO INDIAN BUTTER CHICKEN

Ingredients

150g boneless chicken thighs

2 tablespoons ghee (clarified butter)

2 tablespoons tomato puree

2 tablespoons heavy cream

1 teaspoon garam masala

1/2 teaspoon turmeric

1/4 teaspoon cayenne pepper

Salt to taste

Directions

1   In a pan, heat ghee over medium heat.

2   Add boneless chicken thighs and cook until browned.

3   Reduce the heat and add tomato puree, heavy cream, garam masala, turmeric, cayenne pepper, and salt. Stir well to combine.

4   Cover the pan and simmer for 15-20 minutes, or until the chicken is cooked through and the flavors are well blended.

5   Serve with cauliflower rice or sautéed spinach.

KETO CHEESY CREAMY TOMATO BEEF MEATBALL GRATIN:

Ingredients

450g ground beef

30g almond flour

30g grated Parmesan

30g chopped fresh parsley

30g chopped onion

1 clove garlic, minced

1 egg

5g Italian seasoning

Salt and pepper to taste

For the tomato sauce:

400g crushed tomatoes

60ml heavy cream

5g Italian seasoning

2.5g garlic powder

Salt and pepper to taste

For the gratin topping:

120g mozzarella

30g Parmesan

Directions

1   Preheat the oven to 190°C.

2   Grease a baking dish.

3   Mix all meatball ingredients in a bowl. Shape into meatballs and place in the dish.

4   Combine tomato sauce ingredients and pour over meatballs.

5   Sprinkle with mozzarella and Parmesan cheese.

6   Bake for 25-30 minutes until cooked and cheese is golden. Let it cool before serving.

PALAK PANEER

Directions

1 Heat ghee in a pan and add diced paneer.

2 Cook until the paneer turns golden brown. Remove and set aside.

3 In the same pan, add spinach puree, coconut cream, cumin powder, cinnamon stick, turmeric, and salt. Stir well and let it simmer for 5 minutes.

4 Add the cooked paneer to the spinach mixture and gently mix until well combined.

5 Serve with cucumber raita or a mixed green salad.

Ingredients

150g paneer (Indian cottage cheese)

2 tablespoons ghee

2 cups spinach, blanched and pureed

2 tablespoons coconut cream

1 teaspoon cumin powder

1 cinnamon stick

1/2 teaspoon turmeric

Salt to taste

KETO TANDOORI CHICKEN

Directions

1 Combine Greek yogurt, lemon juice, Tandoori spice mix, olive oil, ground cumin, ground coriander, paprika, turmeric, ground ginger, garlic powder, and salt to make a marinade.

2 Coat chicken thighs with the marinade and refrigerate for at least 2 hours.

3 Grill or bake for 8-10 minutes per side until cooked through.

4 Serve garnished with cilantro (optional) and lemon wedges.

Ingredients

600g chicken drumsticks (skin-on) 8

tablespoons Greek yogurt

4 tablespoons lemon juice

4 teaspoons ginger-garlic paste

4 teaspoons cumin powder

2 teaspoons coriander powder

1 teaspoon paprika

Salt to taste

4 tablespoons Tandoori spice mix

4 tablespoons olive oil

3 teaspoons ground cumin

3 teaspoons turmeric

Fresh cilantro, for garnish (optional)

Lemon wedges, for serving

Salt to taste

EGG CURRY

_____

_____

Ingredients

4 boiled eggs

60 grams coconut oil

240 grams diced tomatoes

120 grams diced onions

10 grams ginger-garlic paste

5 grams cumin powder

5 grams turmeric

2.5 grams chili powder

Salt to taste

Directions

1 Heat oil in a large skillet over medium heat.

2 Sauté onion until translucent and slightly browned.

3 Add garlic, ginger, and spices. Cook for 1 minute until fragrant.

4 Pour in diced tomatoes and cook for a few minutes.

5 Slowly add coconut milk, stirring continuously. Season with salt, pepper, and red pepper flakes (optional).

6 Add hard-boiled eggs to the sauce, ensuring they are submerged.

7 Simmer for 10-15 minutes. Garnish with cilantro before serving.

KETO BAKED SALMON WITH ASPARAGUS

Ingredients

4 salmon fillets

1 bunch asparagus, trimmed

2 tablespoons melted butter

2 cloves garlic, minced

Juice of 1 lemon

Salt and pepper to taste

Directions

1 Preheat the oven to 200°C.

2 Place the salmon fillets and asparagus on a baking sheet.

3 In a small bowl, whisk together the melted butter, minced garlic, lemon juice, salt, and pepper.

4 Drizzle the butter mixture over the salmon and asparagus.

5 Toss the asparagus to coat evenly.

6 Bake for 12-15 minutes until the salmon is cooked through and flakes easily with a fork. Serve the salmon with roasted asparagus.

CAULIFLOWER BIRYANI

Directions

1 Preheat oven to 200°C.

2 Toss cauliflower florets with 1 tbsp ghee or coconut oil. Spread on a lined baking sheet. Roast for 15-20 minutes until tender and golden.

3 In a skillet, sauté onions in 1 tbsp ghee or coconut oil until translucent and slightly browned.

4 Add garlic, ginger, and chili (optional). Cook for 1 minute. Add cumin, coriander, turmeric, chili powder, garam masala, and salt. Mix well. Reduce heat and add Greek yogurt.

5 Stir until spices are coated. Fold in roasted cauliflower. Cook for a few minutes. Remove from heat and garnish with cilantro.

Ingredients

600g cauliflower rice

200g cooked chicken breast (diced)

30g ghee

60g diced onions

60g diced bell peppers

2 tablespoons frozen peas

1/2 teaspoon cumin powder

1/2 teaspoon cardamom powder

1/4 teaspoon cloves

Salt to taste

KETO CAULIFLOWER MAC

AND CHEESE

Directions

1 Preheat the oven to 190°C.

2 Steam or boil the cauliflower florets until tender. Drain well and transfer to a baking dish.

3 In a saucepan, heat the heavy cream over medium heat until hot but not boiling.

4 Add the shredded cheddar cheese and grated Parmesan cheese, stirring until melted and smooth. Stir in the garlic powder, onion powder, salt, and pepper.

5 Pour the cheese sauce over the cauliflower and mix well to coat.

6 Bake for 15-20 minutes until bubbly and golden on top. Serve as a delicious low-carb alternative to traditional mac and cheese.

Ingredients

1 medium cauliflower head, cut into florets

250 ml heavy cream

400 grams shredded cheddar cheese

25 grams grated Parmesan cheese

1/2 teaspoon garlic powder

1/2 teaspoon onion powder

Salt and pepper to taste

KETO BUFFALO CHICKEN DIP

Ingredients

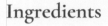

400 grams cooked chicken breast, shredded

120 grams cream cheese

120 grams sour cream

60 ml hot sauce (adjust to taste)

60 ml ranch dressing

120 grams shredded cheddar cheese

30 grams sliced green onions (optional)

Directions

1 Preheat the oven to 175°C.

2 In a mixing bowl, combine the shredded chicken, cream cheese, sour cream, hot sauce, and ranch dressing.

3 Mix well until all ingredients are fully incorporated. Transfer the mixture to a baking dish and spread it evenly.

4 Sprinkle the shredded cheddar cheese on top. Bake for 20-25 minutes until the dip is hot and bubbly, and the cheese is melted and slightly golden.

5 Remove from the oven and garnish with sliced green onions, if desired. Serve with celery sticks or low-carb crackers.

KETO LEMON GARLIC SHRIMP

Ingredients

1 pound shrimp, peeled and deveined

3 tablespoons butter

3 cloves garlic, minced

Juice of 1 lemon

Zest of 1 lemon

Salt and pepper to taste

Chopped fresh parsley, for garnish

Directions

1   In a large skillet, melt the butter over medium heat.

2   Add the minced garlic and cook for 1-2 minutes until fragrant.

3   Add the shrimp to the skillet and cook for 2-3 minutes per side until pink and opaque.

4   Squeeze the lemon juice over the shrimp and sprinkle with lemon zest, salt, and pepper.

5   Stir well to coat the shrimp in the lemon garlic butter sauce. Remove from heat and garnish with chopped fresh parsley. Serve hot.

KETO ZUCCHINI NOODLES

WITH PESTO

Directions

1 Using a spiralizer or julienne peeler, turn the zucchini into noodles. Set aside.

2 In a food processor, combine fresh basil leaves, pine nuts, grated Parmesan cheese, minced garlic, and a pinch of salt and pepper. Pulse until the ingredients are finely chopped.

3 With the food processor running, slowly drizzle in the olive oil until a smooth pesto sauce forms.

4 In a skillet, heat a drizzle of olive oil over medium heat.

5 Add the zucchini noodles and sauté for 2-3 minutes until tender. Remove from heat and toss the noodles with the pesto sauce until well coated. Serve warm.

Ingredients

4 medium zucchini

30 grams fresh basil leaves

30 grams pine nuts

25 grams grated Parmesan cheese

2 cloves garlic, minced

60 ml extra-virgin olive oil

Salt and pepper to taste

KETO SPINACH AND FETA

STUFFED CHICKEN BREAST

Directions

1 Preheat the oven to 190°C.

2 Slice a pocket into each chicken breast without cutting all the way through.

3 In a mixing bowl, combine the thawed spinach, crumbled feta cheese, minced garlic, olive oil, salt, and pepper.

4 Stuff each chicken breast with the spinach and feta mixture. Secure with toothpicks if needed.

5 Place the stuffed chicken breasts on a baking sheet and bake for 25-30 minutes until cooked through and the internal temperature reaches 74°C. Allow the chicken to rest for a few minutes before serving.

Ingredients

600 grams boneless, skinless chicken breasts

150 grams frozen spinach, thawed and drained

75 grams crumbled feta cheese

2 cloves garlic, minced

15 ml olive oil

Salt and pepper to taste

SHAWARMA SPICED CHICKEN

Ingredients

4 boneless, skinless chicken thighs

2 tablespoons olive oil

1 tablespoon ground cumin

1 tablespoon ground coriander

1 teaspoon paprika

1 teaspoon garlic powder

1 teaspoon onion powder

Salt and pepper to taste

Directions

1 In a bowl, combine the olive oil, cumin, coriander, paprika, garlic powder, onion powder, salt, and pepper to make the marinade.

2 Add the chicken thighs to the marinade and coat them well. Let them marinate for at least 30 minutes, or overnight in the refrigerator for more flavor.

3 Preheat the grill or a skillet over medium-high heat. Cook the chicken thighs for about 5-6 minutes per side, or until cooked through.

4 Remove from heat and let the chicken rest for a few minutes. Slice the chicken and serve with a side salad or grilled vegetables. You can also eat with keto arabic bread, made from my book.

SYRIAN SHISH TAWOOK

Ingredients

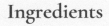

450 g boneless, skinless

chicken breast, cut into cubes

2 tablespoons olive oil

2 tablespoons plain Greek

yogurt

2 cloves garlic, minced

1 tablespoon lemon juice

1 teaspoon paprika

1 teaspoon ground cumin

1/2 teaspoon ground

coriander

Salt and pepper to taste

Directions

1 In a bowl, combine the olive oil, Greek yogurt, minced garlic, lemon juice, paprika, cumin, coriander, salt, and pepper to make the marinade.

2 Add the chicken cubes to the marinade and mix well to ensure they are coated evenly. Let them marinate for at least 30 minutes, or overnight in the refrigerator for maximum flavor.

3 Preheat the grill or a skillet over medium-high heat. Thread the marinated chicken cubes onto skewers.

4 Cook the chicken skewers for about 8-10 minutes, turning occasionally, until they are cooked through and nicely browned.

5 Remove from heat and let the chicken rest for a few minutes before serving. Serve the Shish Tawook with a side of garlic sauce and a salad.

KETO KIBBEH

Directions

1 Prepare the cauliflower (or broccoli) rice by heating it in a skillet over medium heat for about 3-4 minutes. Transfer it to a bowl and let it cool.

2 Blend the onion, parsley, and garlic in a food processor or chop them finely by hand. Transfer the mixture to a large bowl.

3 In a separate bowl, mix the ground beef, onion, garlic, parsley, salt, kibbeh spice mix, and pepper until well combined. Reserve 115 grams of the mixture and leave the rest in the bowl.

4 In a skillet, heat ghee or olive oil and cook the reserved 115 grams of ground beef. Add tomatoes, bell pepper, tomato sauce, pepper, and pine nuts. Cover and simmer until the vegetables are tender. Let it cool.

5 Add ground flaxseed, chia powder, and the cauliflower (or broccoli) rice to the reserved ground beef mixture. Mix well to form a dough.

6 Shape the mixture into oval-shaped balls and create a hollow in the top. Fill the hollow with the cooked meat mixture, sealing it to form the quipes. Repeat until all the mixture is used.

7 Freeze the quipes for 6-8 hours.
Preheat the air fryer to 180°C or the oven to 175°C. Cook the quipes for 25 minutes in the air fryer, flipping them halfway through. If using an oven, cook for 30-40 minutes.

Ingredients

450 grams ground beef

140 g cauliflower or broccoli rice

1 small onion, chopped

Kibbeh spice mix

60 ml tomato sauce (no sugar)

15 grams fresh parsley

1/4 teaspoon pepper

60 grams diced tomatoes

60 grams diced red bell pepper

2 cloves of garlic

2 teaspoons salt

1/2 teaspoon pepper

30 grams pine nuts

30 grams chia powder

60 grams ground flaxseed

Extra virgin olive oil (or ghee)

KETO KOUSA MAHSHI

(STUFFED ZUCCHINI)

Directions

1 Preheat the oven to 190°C.

2 Hollow out the zucchini, reserving the flesh.

3 In a bowl, combine ground meat, cauliflower rice, herbs, onion, garlic, spices, salt, and pepper.

4 Stuff the zucchini shells with the mixture and place in a baking dish.

5 Mix diced tomatoes, tomato paste, and olive oil to create a sauce. Pour the sauce over the zucchini.

6 Bake covered for 45 minutes, then uncover and bake for 15 more minutes until tender. Serve hot, garnished with fresh herbs.

Ingredients

450 grams ground beef or lamb

60 grams cauliflower rice

15 grams chopped fresh parsley

15 grams chopped fresh mint

1 small onion, finely chopped

2 cloves garlic, minced

1 teaspoon ground cumin

1 teaspoon ground coriander

1/2 teaspoon ground cinnamon

1/4 teaspoon ground allspice

Salt and pepper to taste

400 grams diced tomatoes

30 grams tomato paste 2

tablespoons olive oil

KETO BUFFALO CAULIFLOWER BITES

Ingredients

120 grams almond flour

1/2 teaspoon garlic powder

1/2 teaspoon paprika

1/2 teaspoon salt

1/4 teaspoon black pepper

60 ml unsweetened almond

milk

60 ml hot sauce

30 grams melted butter

Directions

1 Preheat the oven to 230°C. In a large bowl, combine the almond flour, garlic powder, paprika, salt, and black pepper.

2 Dip each cauliflower floret into the almond milk, then roll it in the almond flour mixture until well coated.

3 Place the coated florets on a baking sheet lined with parchment paper. Bake for 20-25 minutes until the cauliflower is tender and the coating is crispy.

4 In a separate bowl, mix together the hot sauce and melted butter. Remove the cauliflower from the oven and drizzle the hot sauce mixture over the florets. Toss to coat evenly.

5 Return the baking sheet to the oven and bake for an additional 5 minutes. Remove from the oven and let the buffalo cauliflower bites cool for a few minutes before serving.

6 Serve with your favorite dipping sauce, such as ranch or blue cheese dressing.

CAULIFLOWER CRUST PIZZA

Ingredients

For the crust:

1 medium cauliflower , riced

1 egg

60 g shredded mozzarella

1/2 teaspoon dried oregano

1/4 teaspoon garlic powder

Salt and pepper to taste

For the toppings:

120 ml sugar-free pizza sauce

120 g shredded mozzarella

Your choice of pizza toppings

(e.g., pepperoni, sliced bell

peppers, mushrooms)

Directions

1 Preheat the oven to 220°C. Place the riced cauliflower in a microwave-safe bowl and microwave for 5 minutes.

2 Allow it to cool slightly, then transfer the cauliflower to a clean kitchen towel. Squeeze out as much liquid as possible.

3 In a mixing bowl, combine the cauliflower, egg, shredded mozzarella cheese, dried oregano, garlic powder, salt, and pepper. Mix well until a dough forms.

4 Press the dough onto a parchment-lined baking sheet, shaping it into a round pizza crust. Bake for 15-20 minutes until the crust is golden and firm.

5 Remove from the oven and add the toppings—start with marinara sauce, shredded mozzarella cheese, and your desired toppings.

6 Return the pizza to the oven and bake for an additional 10-15 minutes until the cheese is melted and bubbly. Allow the pizza to cool slightly before slicing and serving.

KETO CHICKEN PARMESAN

Directions

1 Preheat the oven to 190°C.

2 In a shallow bowl, combine almond flour, Parmesan cheese, Italian seasoning, garlic powder, salt, and black pepper. Dredge the chicken breasts in the mixture, pressing it onto both sides.

3 Place the coated chicken breasts on a baking sheet and bake for 20 minutes.

4 Remove from the oven, top each breast with marinara sauce and shredded mozzarella cheese.

5 Return to the oven and bake for an additional 10 minutes or until the cheese is melted and bubbly. Garnish with fresh basil leaves before serving.

Ingredients

2 boneless, skinless chicken breasts

60 grams almond flour

30 grams grated Parmesan cheese

1 teaspoon Italian seasoning

1/2 teaspoon garlic powder

1/4 teaspoon salt

1/4 teaspoon black pepper

60 ml marinara sauce

60 grams shredded mozzarella cheese

Fresh basil leaves, for garnish

STUFFED PORTOBELLO

MUSHROOMS

Directions

1 Preheat the oven to 190°C.

2 Place the Portobello mushrooms on a baking sheet, gill-side up.

3 In a small bowl, combine the ricotta cheese, grated Parmesan cheese, chopped fresh basil, minced garlic, olive oil, salt, and pepper. Mix well.

4 Divide the ricotta mixture evenly among the mushrooms, spreading it over the gills.

5 Bake for 15-20 minutes until the mushrooms are tender and the cheese is golden and bubbly.
Serve a a side dish or as a main course with a side salad.

Ingredients

6 Portobello mushrooms

120 grams ricotta cheese

30 grams grated Parmesan cheese

30 grams chopped fresh basil

2 cloves garlic, minced

30 milliliters olive oil

Salt and pepper to taste

GRILLED LAMB CHOPS WITH GARLIC SAUCE

Ingredients

4 lamb chops

2 tablespoons olive oil

2 cloves garlic, minced

1 teaspoon dried rosemary

1 teaspoon dried thyme

Salt and black pepper to taste

For the Garlic Sauce:

60 mlmayonnaise

2 cloves garlic, minced

1 tablespoon lemon juice

Salt and black pepper to taste

Chopped fresh parsley for garnish

Directions

1 Preheat grill to medium-high heat.

2 In a small bowl, combine olive oil, minced garlic, dried rosemary, dried thyme, salt, and black pepper for the marinade.

3 Coat lamb chops with the marinade and let them marinate for 30 minutes at room temperature or refrigerate for a few hours.

4 Prepare garlic sauce by mixing mayonnaise, minced garlic, lemon juice, salt, and black pepper in a separate bowl.

5 Grill lamb chops for 3-4 minutes per side for medium-rare. Let the lamb chops rest for a few minutes before serving. Serve with garlic sauce and garnish with fresh parsley.

EGYPTIAN–STYLE GRILLED FISH

Ingredients

2 whole fish (such as sea bass
or red snapper), cleaned and
scaled

2 tablespoons olive oil

2 cloves garlic, minced

1 teaspoon ground cumin

1 teaspoon ground coriander

1/2 teaspoon paprika

1/2 teaspoon ground turmeric

Juice of 1 lemon

Salt and pepper to taste

Fresh parsley, chopped (for
garnish)

Lemon wedges, for serving

Directions

1 Preheat the grill to medium-high heat.
In a small bowl, mix together the olive
oil, minced garlic, ground cumin, ground
coriander, paprika, ground turmeric,
lemon juice, salt, and pepper to create a
marinade.

2 Make diagonal cuts on both sides of the
fish, about 1 inch apart.
Rub the marinade all over the fish,
ensuring it gets into the cuts as well. Let
it marinate for at least 30 minutes,
allowing the flavors to penetrate.

3 Place the fish on the preheated grill and
cook for about 4-5 minutes per side, or
until the flesh is opaque and flakes easily
with a fork.

4 Carefully remove the grilled fish from
the grill and transfer it to a serving
platter.
Garnish with fresh parsley and serve
with lemon wedges on the side.

LEBANESE BEEF KOFTA

SKEWERS

Directions

1 In a mixing bowl, combine the ground beef, chopped onion, minced garlic, chopped parsley, ground cumin, ground coriander, paprika, ground cinnamon, salt, and black pepper. Mix well until all the ingredients are evenly incorporated.

2 Divide the mixture into equal portions and shape them into small elongated sausage-like shapes, about 2-3 inches long.

   Preheat the grill or a skillet over medium-high heat. If using a grill, lightly oil the grates.

3 Drizzle the olive oil over the kofta skewers, coating them evenly.

   Grill or cook the kofta skewers for about 3-4 minutes per
4 side, or until they are browned and cooked through.

5 Remove from the heat and let them rest for a few minutes. Serve the Keto Lebanese Beef Kofta Skewers with lemon wedges for squeezing over the top.

Ingredients

200g ground beef

1/2 small onion, finely chopped

1 clove of garlic, minced

2 tablespoons chopped fresh parsley

1/2 teaspoon ground cumin

1/2 teaspoon ground coriander

1/4 teaspoon paprika

1/4 teaspoon ground cinnamon

1/4 teaspoon salt

1/8 teaspoon black pepper

1/2 tablespoon olive oil (for

cooking)

Lemon wedges, for serving

MOROCCAN SPICED

CHICKEN TAGINE

Directions

1 Heat the olive oil in a large skillet or tajine over medium heat. Season the chicken breasts with salt and pepper, then add them to the skillet.

2 Cook until browned on both sides. Remove the chicken and set aside. In the same skillet, add the diced onion and minced garlic.
Sauté until the onion is softened and translucent.
Add the spices. Stir well to coat the onions and garlic with the spices.

3 Add the zucchini slices, and bell peppers to the skillet. Cook for a few minutes until slightly softened. Return the chicken breasts to the skillet, along with any juices that may have accumulated.

4 Add the diced tomatoes and chicken broth.
Cover the skillet or transfer the mixture to a tajine pot if you have one. Simmer for about 25-30 minutes, or until the chicken is cooked through and the flavors have melded together.
Add the pitted green olives and chopped fresh cilantro to the tajine. Stir gently to incorporate.

5 Adjust the seasoning with salt and pepper according to your taste.
Serve the Keto Moroccan Style Chicken Tajine hot, garnished with additional cilantro if desired.

Ingredients

2 chicken breasts, boneless and skinless

2 tablespoons olive oil

1 onion, diced

3 cloves garlic, minced

1 teaspoon ground cumin

1 teaspoon ground coriander

1 teaspoon ground paprika

1/2 teaspoon ground turmeric

1/2 teaspoon ground cinnamon

1/4 teaspoon ground ginger

1/4 teaspoon cayenne pepper (optional)

1 cup zucchini, sliced

1 cup bell peppers, sliced

1 cup diced tomatoes

1 cup chicken broth

10 green olives, pitted

2 tablespoons chopped fresh cilantro

Salt and pepper to taste

SAUDI-STYLE GRILLED CHICKEN WINGS

Ingredients

700 g chicken wings

2 tablespoons olive oil

2 tablespoons lemon juice

2 cloves garlic, minced

1 teaspoon ground cumin

1 teaspoon ground coriander

1/2 teaspoon ground paprika

1/2 teaspoon ground turmeric

1/4 teaspoon ground

cinnamon

Salt and pepper to taste

Directions

1 Preheat the grill to medium-high heat.

2 In a bowl, mix together olive oil, lemon juice, minced garlic, cumin, coriander, paprika, turmeric, cinnamon, salt, and pepper to make a marinade.

3 Coat the chicken wings evenly with the marinade and let them marinate for at least 30 minutes (or overnight in the refrigerator).

4 Remove the wings from the marinade, shaking off any excess.

5 Grill the wings for 15-20 minutes, turning occasionally, until they are cooked through and crispy. Baste the wings with the remaining marinade while grilling.

6 Serve the Chicken Wings with salad

MOLOKHIA

Ingredients

½ kg of molokhia leaves

1 whole chicken.

2 sticks cinnamon.

2 leaves of laurel.

4 cardamom pods.

1 cup chopped green

coriander.

1 cup peeled garlic.

2 peeled onions.

3 teaspoons dry coriander.

½ teaspoon soft cinnamon.

1 teaspoon salt.

1 pinch black pepper.

5 tablespoons vegetable oil.

1 lemon.

1 hot green pepper

Directions

1   Wash and dry the molokhia leaves.

2   Boil the chicken with cinnamon stick, bay leaf, and cardamom pods until tender.

3   In a saucepan, sauté garlic, onions, and pepper with vegetable oil. Add dried coriander, chopped green coriander, and salt. Stir well. Add molokhia leaves to the pan and cook while stirring, adding lemon juice to prevent elasticity.
Reduce heat and continue stirring until chicken is cooked.

4   Pour chicken broth into the pan, ensuring chicken is submerged, and let it boil. Reduce heat and simmer for half an hour until molokhia becomes tender.

5   Transfer the cooked molokhia to a serving dish.
Remove chicken bones and skin, and place chicken pieces over the molokhia.
Serve with cauliflower rice.

MIDDLE EASTERN ZUCCHINI

BOATS

Directions

1 Preheat the oven to 190°C.

2 Cut the zucchini in half lengthwise and scoop out the seeds to form zucchini boats.

3 Sauté diced onion and minced garlic in a skillet with 1 tablespoon of olive oil until translucent.
Add ground beef, cumin, coriander, paprika, cinnamon, salt, and pepper to the skillet. Cook until the beef is browned.

4 Remove the skillet from heat and mix in diced tomatoes and chopped parsley. Brush the zucchini boats with the remaining olive oil and place them on a baking sheet.

5 Fill each boat with the ground beef mixture.

6 Bake in the preheated oven for 20-25 minutes, until the zucchini is tender and the filling is cooked through. Add crumbled feta cheese during the last few minutes of baking.

Ingredients

2 medium zucchini

200 grams ground beef

1/4 cup diced onion

2 cloves garlic, minced

1/2 teaspoon ground cumin

1/2 teaspoon ground coriander

1/2 teaspoon ground paprika

1/4 teaspoon ground cinnamon

Salt and pepper to taste

2 tablespoons olive oil

1/4 cup diced tomatoes

2 tablespoons chopped fresh parsley

2 tablespoons crumbled feta cheese

KETO SYRIAN BAMIA

Directions

1 Heat the olive oil in a large skillet or frying pan, add the onions, and cook over low heat, stirring occasionally, for 5 minutes until softened but not
2 colored.

Add the garlic and cook for another minute.
Add the lamb, increase the heat to medium, and cook, stirring frequently, for 8–10 minutes until evenly
3 browned.

Put the okra into a roasting pan, drizzle with a little olive oil, and roast for 30 minutes.
4

Pour enough boiling water into the pan of lamb to cover and cook for 30 minutes.

5 Stir in the tomato paste , okra, and seven spices seasoning and continue to cook for 1 hour more or until the sauce has reduced and thickened and the lamb is tender.
Season with salt and pepper.
Serve with cauliflower rice.

Ingredients

2 tablespoons olive oil, plus extra

for drizzling

2 small onions, finely chopped

5 garlic cloves, sliced

400 g boneless lamb, diced

450 g okra, trimmed

3 tablespoons tomato paste (purée)

½ teaspoon seven spices seasoning

salt and pepper

SLOW COOKER MISSISSIPPI POT ROAST

Ingredients

1.5 kg beef roast (either

chuck roast or outside round)

300 g beef broth

5 chili peppers

120 grams butter

1 teaspoon dried parsley

1/2 teaspoon onion powder

1/2 teaspoon garlic powder

1/2 teaspoon black pepper

1/2 teaspoon dried dill weed

Salt to taste

Directions

1   Combine the dried seasonings in a small bowl. Massage the outside of the beef roast with the seasonings. Place it in the bottom of a 6-liter slow cooker.

2   Pour the beef broth into the sides of the slow cooker. Add the chili peppers. Place the butter on top of the beef, cover, and cook on low for 8-10 hours or on high for 4-5 hours, or until the beef is fork-tender.

3   Remove the beef from the slow cooker and, using a fork, gently pull apart large chunks of beef. Stir them into the juices.

4   Serve the beef over mashed cauliflower and drizzle with the juices from the slow cooker.

LOW CARB ENCHILADAS

Ingredients

1/2 onion, diced

1 jalapeno, minced

1 can enchilada sauce, divided

400 grams cooked chicken

200 grams cheddar cheese

8 low carb tortillas

Directions

1   Preheat oven to 200°C.

2   Sautee onions and jalapenos together over medium heat until tender.

3   Add enchilada sauce to the tortillas and add chicken, cheese, and onion mixture to them.

4   Roll up tortillas with the seam on the bottom and place in a 9x13 pan.

5   Pour remaining sauce on top and remaining cheese.

6   Bake for 20 minutes covered and then 5 minutes uncovered.

CREAMY TUSCAN

CHICKEN SKILLET

Directions

1 Cut the cauliflower into bite-sized pieces. Simmer the cauliflower in chicken broth for 5-6 minutes until tender-crisp. Remove the cauliflower and reserve the broth.

2 Season the chicken with Italian seasoning, salt, and pepper.

3 Heat oil in a large skillet and brown the chicken. Remove and set aside.

4 In the same skillet, cook garlic until fragrant. Add 1/2 cup of the reserved cauliflower broth, cream, and sundried tomatoes. Simmer until thickened.

5 Reduce heat to medium-low. Add chicken, cauliflower, spinach, and Parmesan cheese. Cook for 2-3 minutes until the sauce thickens and everything is heated through.

6 Season with salt and pepper to taste. Garnish with fresh basil and additional Parmesan, if desired.

Ingredients

1 large head cauliflower

250 ml chicken broth

180 g boneless, chicken breasts

1 teaspoon Italian seasoning

Salt and pepper to taste

1 tablespoon olive oil, or as needed

2 cloves garlic, minced

350 ml heavy cream

80 g grated Parmesan cheese

60 grams sundried tomatoes

40 g fresh spinach leaves

PIZZA BOWL

Directions

1 Preheat oven to 230°C.

2 Heat oil in a pan over medium-high heat. Add garlic, green pepper, and mushrooms. Cook until tender, about 5 minutes.

3 Stir in cauliflower rice, oregano, and basil. Cook until cauliflower is cooked through.

4 Divide the mixture over 4 oven-safe bowls. Top with pizza sauce, cooked sausage, pepperoni, olives, and cheeses.

5 Bake for 15 minutes or until cheese is browned and bubbly. Top with fresh herbs if desired.

Ingredients

1 tablespoon olive oil

2 cloves garlic

150 grams green bell pepper, diced

150 grams mushrooms, sliced

360 grams cauliflower rice

0.5 teaspoon oregano

0.25 teaspoon basil

240 ml low carb pizza sauce

225 grams turkey sausage

30 grams halal salami slices

1 tablespoon black olives (optional)

200 grams shredded mozzarella

30 grams Parmesan cheese

KETO GNOCCHI

Ingredients

40 g grated mozzarella cheese

80 g Mascarpone

130 g almond flour

1 egg

Salt to taste

Directions

1 Heat the mozzarella cheese with the mascarpone in the microwave until melted together. Take it out every 15 - 20 seconds and stir. Add the egg and mix thoroughly. Sprinkle in the almond flour and salt.

2 Knead the dough until it comes together nicely. Consider that not all almond flours are the same, so you may need to add more flour to achieve the right consistency.

3 Divide the dough into 4 portions. Roll each portion into long strips, then cut them into 2 cm pieces. Shape each piece individually into a ball, then roll it along the back of a fork to create the characteristic gnocchi shape.

4 Use the prepared dough by either sautéing it in a pan or boiling it in salted water.

5 Serve it with any kind of meat or vegetable sauce. Enjoy your meal!

MINI KETO HOTDOGS

Ingredients

180g shredded mozzarella

56g mascarpone

140g almond flour

1 tsp garlic powder

14g coconut flour

Salt , Pepper to taste

1 tablespoon baking powder

1 large egg

8 hot dog sausages

For topping: Cheese to taste

Igrated cheese on top of each

wrapped sausage.

Directions

1 In a bowl, whisk together the coconut flour, eggs, almond milk, baking powder, and sweetener until well combined.

2 Heat butter or coconut oil in a non-stick skillet over medium heat.

3 Spoon the pancake batter onto the skillet, forming small pancakes.

4 Cook for 2-3 minutes on each side until golden brown.

5 Serve the pancakes with your choice of toppings, such as sugar-free syrup or berries.

CRISPY–TENDER DUCK LEG

WITH CELERY PUREE

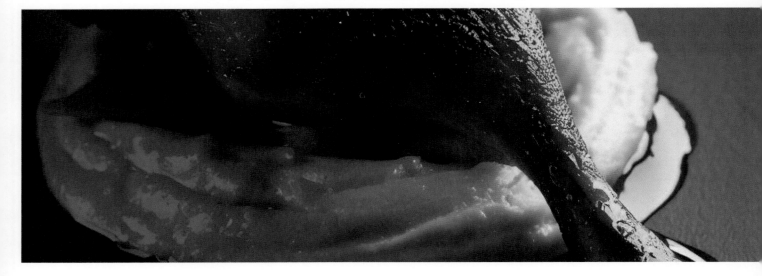

Directions

1   Slice the onions and place them at the bottom of a baking dish. Add garlic on top. Optionally, add 4-5 bay leaves.

2   Clean the duck legs and season the lower part with salt, pepper, rosemary, thyme, and marjoram. Place the seasoned duck legs tightly on top of the onions in the baking dish.

3   Pour approximately 6-8 dl of water over the duck legs. Season the skin with salt and pepper, then cover the dish with aluminum foil. Bake in a preheated oven at 150 degrees Celsius for 4 hours.

4   Peel and cook the celery for the celery puree. Once tender, transfer the cooked celery to a blender, add a little bit of the cooking liquid, and blend until smooth. Pour it into a bowl.

5   Add cream cheese and mix well using a hand mixer or electric whisk. Season with salt and pepper to taste. Add butter and mix well.

6   30 minutes before serving, transfer the duck legs to a larger baking dish (lined with parchment paper) along with some onions. Roast at 210 degrees Celsius until crispy.

Ingredients

4 duck legs

4 onions

8 cloves of garlic

Salt and pepper to taste

Rosemary , Thyme, Marjoram to taste

For the celery puree

1 kg of celery

Salt to taste

Pepper to taste

3 large tablespoons of cream cheese 5-10 grams of butter

ROSEMARY CHICKEN LIVER

WITH MUSHROOMS

Directions

1 Clean and slice the mushrooms and onion.

2 Heat the goose fat in a skillet and add the mushrooms and onions. Sauté them for a while.

3 Then season to taste and add the washed and drained chicken liver.

4 Mix everything together and add the peeled garlic cloves. Cover and simmer until cooked. Do not add water as the mushrooms release enough liquid.

5 Serve with celery puree.

Ingredients

500g chicken liver

500g mushrooms

1bigger onion

2 tablespoons goose fat

Salt Pepper

Rosemary

5-6 cloves of garlic

KETO NOODLES

Ingredients

60 grams Cream Cheese

30 grams Butter

24 grams Almond Flour

3 Eggs

5 grams Turmeric

Salt to taste

Directions

1 Set the oven temperature to 150°C. Prepare a baking tray and line it with an oiled baking paper or silicon sheet.

2 Combine all the ingredients in a kitchen mixer and blend until smooth. Pour the mixture onto the prepared baking tray.

3 Using a spatula or knife, spread the mixture evenly, ensuring it is as thin as possible. Place the tray in the oven and bake for 8 minutes.

4 After baking, allow the pasta sheet to cool, then carefully roll it into a log shape.

5 Using a sharp knife, cut the rolled pasta into your desired pasta size.

6 Unroll the cut pieces and transfer them to a serving bowl. They are now ready to be served. No need to cook.

DESSERTS

KETO CHOCOLATE CHIP COOKIES

Ingredients

240 g almond flour

60 g coconut flour

120 g granulated sweetener

(such as erythritol)

1/2 teaspoon baking soda

1/4 teaspoon salt

120 g melted coconut oil

60 g sugar-free chocolate

chips

1 teaspoon vanilla extract

2 large eggs

Directions

1   Preheat the oven to 175°C.

2   In a mixing bowl, whisk together the flours, sweetener, baking soda, and salt. In a separate bowl, combine the melted coconut oil, sugar-free chocolate chips, vanilla extract, and eggs. Mix until well combined. Add the wet ingredients to the dry ingredients and stir until a dough forms.

3

4   Fold in any additional chocolate chips if desired. Drop spoonfuls of dough onto a baking sheet lined with parchment paper. Flatten each cookie slightly with the back of a spoon.

5   Bake for 10-12 minutes until golden around the edges. Remove from the oven and let the cookies cool on the baking sheet for a few minutes, then transfer them to a wire rack to cool completely.

KETO CHEESECAKE

Ingredients

For the crust:

180 grams almond flour

56 grams melted butter

28 grams granulated
sweetener (such as erythritol)

For the filling:

680 grams cream cheese,
softened

150 grams granulated
sweetener (such as erythritol)

3 large eggs

5 grams vanilla extract

For the topping:

120 grams sour cream

15 grams lemon juice

6 grams grated lemon zest

2 grams vanilla extract

Directions

1 Preheat the oven to 165°C.

2 Mix almond flour, melted butter, and
   granulated sweetener for the crust. Press the
   mixture into a 25 cm springform pan and bake
   for 10 minutes.

3 In a separate bowl, beat cream cheese,
   sweetener, eggs, vanilla extract, sour cream,
   lemon juice, and lemon zest until smooth.

4 Pour the filling over the crust and bake for 45-50
   minutes.

5 Let the cheesecake cool in the oven for 1 hour,
   then refrigerate for at least 4 hours before
   serving.

GREEK YOGURT PARFAIT

Directions

1 In a bowl or glass, layer the Greek yogurt, mixed berries, chopped nuts, and shredded coconut.

2 Repeat the layers if desired.

Ingredients

120 grams Greek yogurt

30 grams mixed berries (e.g., strawberries, blueberries)

15 grams chopped nuts (e.g., almonds, walnuts)

15 grams unsweetened shredded coconut

KETO AVOCADO CHOCOLATE

MOUSSE

Directions

1 In a blender or food processor, combine the avocados, cocoa powder, powdered sweetener, almond milk, vanilla extract, and salt. Blend until smooth and creamy.

2 If the mixture is too thick, add more almond milk, a tablespoon at a time, until desired consistency is reached.

3 Taste and adjust the sweetness if needed.

4 Transfer the mousse to serving dishes or glasses.

5 Refrigerate for at least 1-2 hours to set.

6 Before serving, garnish with whipped cream and grated dark chocolate if desired.

Ingredients

2 ripe avocados, peeled and pitted

25 grams unsweetened cocoa powder

48 grams powdered sweetener (such as erythritol)

60 ml unsweetened almond milk 1 teaspoon vanilla extract

 Pinch of salt

Whipped cream and grated dark chocolate for garnish (optional)

KETO COCONUT FLOUR BROWNIES

Ingredients

30 g coconut flour: 4

0 g cocoa powder

1/2 teaspoon baking soda

1/4 teaspoon salt

2 large eggs

180 g peanut butter

60 ml keto maple syrup

1 teaspoon vanilla extract

65 g sweetener of choice

180 g chocolate chips

Directions

1   In a bowl, combine the natural peanut butter, melted coconut oil, unsweetened cocoa powder, powdered erythritol (or sweetener of choice), and vanilla extract. Mix well until all the ingredients are thoroughly combined.

2   Spoon the mixture into silicone molds or an ice cube tray, distributing it evenly. Place the molds or tray in the freezer and let them freeze for 1-2 hours or until they become firm.

3   Once firm, remove the fat bombs from the molds and transfer them to an airtight container.

4   Store the fat bombs in the freezer in the airtight container to keep them fresh and ready to enjoy whenever you want a tasty treat.

KETO LEMON BARS

Ingredients

115 grams butter, melted

290 grams almond flour

120 grams powdered
erythritol

3 medium lemons

3 large eggs

Directions

1. In a mixing bowl, combine melted butter, 200 g almond flour, 30 grams of erythritol, and a pinch of salt. Mix well until the ingredients form a crumbly mixture.

2.

3. Press the mixture evenly into an 8x8" baking dish lined with parchment paper. Bake the crust in a preheated oven at 180 degrees Celsius for 20 minutes. After baking, let it cool for 10 minutes.

4.

5. In a separate bowl, zest one lemon and then juice all three lemons. Add the eggs, 90 grams of erythritol, 90 grams of almond flour, and a pinch of salt to the bowl. Mix well to combine and create the filling.

Pour the filling onto the cooled crust in the baking dish, spreading it evenly. Bake in the oven for 25 minutes. Once baked, let it cool and serve.

KETO PEANUT BUTTER

CHOCOLATE FAT BOMBS

Directions

1 In a bowl, mix together the peanut butter, melted coconut oil, cocoa powder, powdered erythritol, and vanilla extract until well combined.

2 Spoon the mixture into silicone molds or an ice cube tray. Freeze for 1-2 hours or until firm.

3 Remove the fat bombs from the molds and store in an airtight container in the freezer.

Ingredients

120 g natural peanut butter (sugar-free)

60 g coconut oil, melted

2 tablespoons unsweetened cocoa powder

2 tablespoons powdered erythritol or

sweetener of choice

1/2 teaspoon vanilla extract

KETO VANILLA CHEESECAKE BITES

Directions

1 Preheat the oven to 175°C and line a mini muffin tin with paper liners.

2 In a bowl, mix together the almond flour, powdered erythritol, and melted butter to form the crust mixture. Press the crust mixture into the bottom of each paper liner in the mini muffin tin.

3 In a separate bowl, beat the cream cheese, powdered erythritol, and vanilla extract until smooth. Add the egg and continue to beat until well combined.

4 Spoon the cheesecake filling over the crust in each paper liner, filling almost to the top.

5 Bake for 15-18 minutes or until the cheesecake is set and slightly golden. Remove from the oven and allow the cheesecake bites to cool completely before serving.

Ingredients

For the crust:

120 grams almond flour

16 grams powdered erythritol or sweetener of choice

42 grams melted butter

For the filling:

225 grams cream cheese, softened

30 grams powdered erythritol or sweetener of choice

2.5 milliliters vanilla extract

1 large egg

KETO BLUEBERRY MUG CAKE

Ingredients

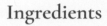

2 tablespoons almond flour

1 tablespoon coconut flour

1 tablespoon powdered erythritol or sweetener of choice

1/4 teaspoon baking powder

Pinch of salt

1 tablespoon melted butter

1 large egg

1/4 teaspoon vanilla extract

2 tablespoons fresh blueberries

Directions

1   In a microwave-safe mug, whisk together the almond flour, coconut flour, powdered erythritol, baking powder, and salt.

2   Add the melted butter, egg, and vanilla extract to the mug. Mix until well combined.

3   Gently fold in the fresh blueberries.

4   Microwave the mug on high for 1-2 minutes or until the cake is set in the center. Allow the mug cake to cool for a few minutes before enjoying.

KETO CINNAMON ROLLS

Ingredients

For the dough:

240 grams almond flour

30 grams coconut flour

48 grams sweetener of choice

10 grams baking powder

2 grams xanthan gum

1 gram salt

3 large eggs

56 grams melted butter

10 ml vanilla extract

For the filling:

28 grams melted butter

24 grams sweetener of choice

4 grams ground cinnamon

For the cream cheese frosting:

113 g cream cheese, softened

28 grams sweetener of choice

15 ml heavy cream

2.5 ml vanilla extract

Directions

1 Preheat oven to 175°C and line a baking dish with parchment paper.

2 In a mixing bowl, whisk almond flour, coconut flour, granulated erythritol, baking powder, xanthan gum, and salt. In a separate bowl, whisk eggs, melted butter, and vanilla extract together.

3 Pour the wet ingredients into the dry ingredients and stir to form a dough. Roll out the dough between two sheets of parchment paper into a rectangle.

4 In a small bowl, mix melted butter, granulated erythritol, and ground cinnamon for the filling. Spread the filling mixture evenly over the rolled-out dough. Roll the dough tightly into a log shape, starting from one end. Slice the log into 8 equal-sized rolls and place them in the prepared baking dish. Bake for 20-25 minutes until the rolls are golden brown and firm.

5 While the rolls are baking, prepare the cream cheese frosting by beating softened cream cheese, powdered erythritol, heavy cream, and vanilla extract together until smooth. Remove the rolls from the oven and let them cool slightly before drizzling the cream cheese frosting over the top.

KETO COCONUT

MACAROONS

Directions

1 Preheat the oven to 200°C. Line a 23 x 33 cm cookie sheet with parchment paper and set it aside.

2 In a large bowl, mix together the almond flour, shredded coconut, coconut oil or butter, and vanilla extract. Set the mixture aside.

3 Using the whisk attachment on your stand mixer, beat the egg whites and Swerve together until stiff peaks form.

4 Gently fold the beaten egg whites into the almond flour mixture. Using a spoon, scoop the mixture onto the prepared cookie sheet to form 10-12 mounds.

5 Bake for 15-16 minutes, or until the tops of the coconut macaroons start to lightly brown.

6 Remove from the oven and let them cool before removing them from the cookie sheet.

Ingredients

30 grams Superfine Almond Flour

185 grams Unsweetened Shredded Coconut

1 tablespoon vanilla extract

15 grams Butter

4 egg whites

45 grams Sweetener of choice

KETO PIE

Directions

1 Preheat your oven to 175°C and grease a pie dish.

2 In a mixing bowl, combine the almond flour, coconut flour, granulated erythritol, and salt for the crust.
Add the melted butter and egg to the dry ingredients. Mix well until a dough forms.

3 Press the dough evenly into the bottom and up the sides of the greased pie dish.

4 In a separate bowl, whisk together the heavy cream, powdered erythritol, eggs, and vanilla extract for the filling.
Pour the filling into the prepared crust.

5 Bake in the preheated oven for 35-40 minutes, or until the center of the pie is set.

6 Remove from the oven and let the pie cool completely before serving.

7 If desired, top with whipped cream and berries before serving.

Ingredients

180 grams almond flour

30 grams coconut flour

48 grams granulated sweetener of choice

2 grams salt

56 grams melted butter

1 large egg

For the filling:

480 milliliters heavy cream

90 grams powdered sweetener of choice

4 large eggs

5 milliliters vanilla extract

For the topping (optional):

Whipped cream

Berries

PISTACHIO CARDAMO M COOKIES

Ingredients

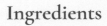

120 grams almond flour

60 grams unsalted butter,

softened

245 g powdered erythritol

2 grams ground cardamom

30 grams chopped pistachios

Directions

1 Preheat oven to 175°C and line a baking sheet with parchment paper.

2 In a mixing bowl, combine almond flour, softened butter, powdered erythritol, and ground cardamom. Mix well.

3 Shape the dough into small cookies, placing them on the prepared baking sheet.

4 Press chopped pistachios onto each cookie and bake for 10-12 minutes until lightly golden.
   Allow to cool before serving.

CARDAMOM ROSEWATER CHIA PUDDING

Ingredients

240 ml unsweetened almond milk

3 tablespoons chia seeds

2.5 grams ground cardamom

2.5 grams rosewater

12 grams powdered erythritol (optional)

Sliced almonds and dried rose petals for garnish

Directions

1 In a jar or bowl, combine almond milk, chia seeds, ground cardamom, rosewater, and powdered erythritol (if using).Stir well to combine all the ingredients.

2 Cover the jar or bowl and refrigerate overnight or for at least 4 hours until the chia seeds have absorbed the liquid and the pudding has thickened.

3 Stir the pudding before serving and adjust the sweetness if desired.

4 Garnish with sliced almonds and dried rose petals.Enjoy chilled.

LEBANESE ORANGE BLOSSOM

PANNA COTTA

Directions

1 In a small saucepan, heat the heavy cream over low heat until hot but not boiling.

2 In a separate bowl, combine water and gelatin. Let it bloom for a few minutes.

3 Add the bloomed gelatin and powdered erythritol to the hot cream, stirring until fully dissolved.

4 Remove from heat and stir in the orange blossom water.

5 Pour the mixture into ramekins or molds and refrigerate for at least 4 hours or until set. Serve chilled.

Ingredients

240 ml heavy cream

60 ml water

15 grams powdered gelatin

48 grams powdered erythritol

5 milliliters orange blossom water

ARABIC COFFEE MOUSSE

Directions

1 In a small saucepan, heat the heavy cream, powdered erythritol, Arabic coffee, and ground cardamom over low heat, stirring until the mixture is hot but not boiling.

2 In a separate bowl, combine the gelatin powder and water. Let it bloom for a few minutes.

3 Add the bloomed gelatin to the hot cream mixture, stirring until fully dissolved.

4 Remove from heat and strain the mixture to remove any coffee grounds.

5 Pour the mixture into serving glasses or bowls and refrigerate for at least 4 hours or until set.
Serve chilled.

Ingredients

240 ml heavy cream

2 tablespoons powdered erythritol

2 tablespoons Arabic coffee (finely ground)

1/2 teaspoon ground cardamom

1 teaspoon gelatin powder

2 tablespoons water

BAKLAVA FAT BOMBS

Ingredients

120 grams almond flour

60 grams unsalted butter,

melted

2 tablespoons powdered

erythritol

1/2 teaspoon ground

cinnamon

30 grams chopped walnuts

30 grams chopped pistachios

Sugar-free honey substitute

for drizzling (optional)

Directions

1   In a mixing bowl, combine almond flour, melted butter, powdered erythritol, and ground cinnamon. Mix well.

2   Add the chopped walnuts and pistachios to the mixture and stir until evenly distributed.

3   Shape the mixture into small balls or squares and place them on a baking sheet lined with parchment paper. Freeze for 1-2 hours until firm.

4   Drizzle with sugar-free honey substitute, if desired, before serving. Enjoy chilled.

PISTACHIO
ROSEWATER
ICE CREAM

Ingredients

480 ml heavy cream

240 ml unsweetened almond
milk

120 grams powdered
erythritol

120 grams chopped pistachios

1 teaspoon rosewater

Directions

1   In a mixing bowl, combine heavy cream,
almond milk, powdered erythritol,
chopped pistachios, and rosewater. Mix
well.

2   Pour the mixture into an ice cream
maker and churn according to the
manufacturer's instructions.

3   Transfer the churned ice cream to a
lidded container and freeze for a few
hours until firm.

4   Serve chilled.

ROSE CARDAMOM YOGURT

PARFAIT

Directions

1 In a bowl, combine Greek yogurt, powdered erythritol, rosewater, and ground cardamom. Mix well.

2 Layer the yogurt mixture with chopped pistachios in serving glasses or bowls.

3 Repeat the layers until all the ingredients are used, ending with a layer of chopped pistachios on top.

4 Refrigerate for at least 1 hour to allow the flavors to meld together.Serve chilled.

Ingredients

240 g full-fat Greek yogurt

1 tablespoon powdered erythritol

1/2 teaspoon rosewater

1/4 teaspoon ground cardamom

Chopped pistachios for topping

ARABIC ALMOND COOKIES

Directions

1 Preheat oven to 165°C and line a baking sheet with parchment paper.

2 In a mixing bowl, combine almond flour, powdered erythritol, ground cinnamon, ground nutmeg, and ground cloves. Mix well.

3 Add melted butter and vanilla extract to the dry ingredients. Stir until the dough comes together. Roll the dough into small balls and place them on the prepared baking sheet.

4 Flatten each ball slightly with the palm of your hand. Press a sliced almond on top of each cookie. Bake for 12-15 minutes until golden brown.

5 Allow to cool before serving.

Ingredients

240 grams almond flour

60 grams powdered erythritol

1 teaspoon ground cinnamon

1/4 teaspoon ground nutmeg

1/4 teaspoon ground cloves

1/4 cup unsalted butter, melted

1 teaspoon vanilla extract

Sliced almonds for topping

KETO TÚRÓGOMBÓC (HUNGARIAN COTTAGE CHEESE DUMPLINGS)

Ingredients

50g full-fat cottage cheese

2 tablespoons almond flour

1 tablespoon coconut flour

1 large egg

1/2 teaspoon vanilla extract

1 tablespoon powdered

erythritol (or your preferred

keto-friendly sweetener)

cocnut oil and psyllium husk

for coating the dumplings

Optional: Lemon zest for

garnish

Directions

1   In a bowl, combine the cottage cheese, almond flour, coconut flour, egg, vanilla extract, and powdered erythritol. Mix well until all the ingredients are thoroughly combined. Place the mixture in the refrigerator for 15-20 minutes to firm up.

2   While the dough is chilling, bring a pot of water to a gentle simmer. Once the dough has firmed up, remove it from the refrigerator.

3   Wet your hands with water to prevent sticking and shape the dough into small dumplings. Gently drop the dumplings into the simmering water and cook for about 8-10 minutes, or until they float to the surface.

4   Sauté the psyllium husk in some coconut oil in a pan until golden brown. Transfer to a plate. Using a slotted spoon, carefully remove the dumplings from the water and place them on the psyhllium husk and coat them.

5   Optional: Garnish the túrógombóc with a sprinkle of lemon zest for extra flavor. Serve the túrógombóc warm as is or with a drizzle of melted butter or a dollop of sweet sour cream.

KETO VANILLA ICE CREAM

Ingredients

250ml milk

250ml cream

Vanilla extract or 2 vanilla

sticks or stevia vanilla sugar

4 egg yolks

Stevia

Directions

1 Heat milk with vanilla until it boils, then simmer for 30 minutes.

2 Take out the vanilla sticks and cut out the seeds and add them to the milk.

3 Beat egg yolks in a separate bowl. Slowly pour milk into yolks while stirring.

4 Return mixture to pan and bring to a boil. Remove from heat and let cool.

5 Add stevia. Chill a bowl in the freezer. Mix cream into cooled mixture and pour into ice cream machine.

6 Transfer churned ice cream to chilled bowl. Add desired toppings. Freeze for a few hours or overnight.

KETO KAISERSCHMARRN

Directions

1. n a large mixing bowl, whisk the egg yolks, almond flour, coconut flour, erythritol, vanilla extract, and salt until well combined. In a separate bowl, beat the egg whites until stiff peaks form.

2. Gently fold the beaten egg whites into the yolk mixture until fully incorporated.

3. Heat butter in a non-stick skillet over medium heat. Pour the batter into the skillet and spread it out evenly. Cook for a few minutes until the bottom is golden brown, then flip the pancake over.

4. Use a spatula or spoon to tear the pancake into small pieces (traditional for Kaiserschmarrn). Continue cooking until the pieces are golden brown and cooked through.

5. Remove from heat and serve the Kaiserschmarrn warm. Sprinkle with powdered erythritol if desired and serve with sugar-free syrup and berries on top.

Ingredients

4 large eggs, separated

30 grams almond flour

20 grams coconut flour

20 grams erythritol (or any keto-friendly sweetener)

1/2 teaspoon vanilla extract

Pinch of salt

30 grams butter

Optional toppings: powdered erythritol, sugar-free syrup, berries

KETO CHOCOLATE CAKE

Directions

1 Preheat the oven to 180 degrees Celsius.

2 The Sponge: Separate and beat the egg whites. Mix the remaining ingredients with the egg yolks. Gently fold in the egg whites.

3 Line the cake pan with baking paper and grease the sides with butter. Pour the batter into the pan and bake for 15-20 minutes. Allow it to cool and then cut it in half.

4 The Cream : Beat the cream with stevia.

5 Mix the room temperature mascarpone with stevia, vanilla extract and mix with a blender.

6 Put the chocolate in a heatproof bowl.
Place bowl over a saucepan of simmering water.

7 Then add the melted chocolate to the mascarpone and stir together. Add the beaten cream to the mascarpone.

8 Put filling on one of the sponges then put the other one on the top and add the rest of the filling to the top and sides.
Put it in the fridge for a night.

Ingredients

Ingredients for the sponge (22cm)

4 eggs

Pinch of salt

Sweetener

2 tbsp cocoa powder

Milk

6 tbsp almond flour

Half pack of baking powder

Vanilla extract

Ingredients for the filling:

70g 80% dark chocolate

Sweetener

Vanilla extract

1 pack of mascarpone

200ml cream

KETO CREPES

Ingredients

10 eggs

Pinch of salt

vanilla

Stevia

150g cream cheese

1 tsp cinnamon

Coconut oil for cooking

Directions

1 Blend all ingredients except the coconut oil in a blender.

2 Cook the mixture on a griddle.

3 Flip when the sides start to turn golden brown.

4 Fill with your choice of ingredients.

KETO GULAB JAMUN

Ingredients

For the gulab jamuns :

80 grams almond flour

1 teaspoon xanthan gum

1/2 teaspoon baking powder

200 grams cottage

cheese/paneer

Sugar Syrup:

200 grams sweetener

180 ml water

A few strands of saffron

A few drops of saffron color

1/2 teaspoon lemon juice

Ghee for frying

Directions

1 In a bowl, mix together the almond flour, xanthan gum, baking powder, and cottage cheese/paneer until well combined.

2 Grease your hands with oil to prevent sticking, then shape the mixture into small balls.

3 Heat ghee in a deep pan or skillet over medium heat. Carefully add the formed balls to the hot ghee and fry them until they turn golden brown, stirring gently to ensure even cooking. Remove the fried balls and set them aside.

4 In a separate saucepan, prepare the sugar syrup by combining xylitol sugar-free (or any similar sweetener), water, saffron strands, saffron color, and lemon juice. Bring the mixture to a gentle boil, stirring occasionally to dissolve the sweetener.

5 Once the sugar syrup is ready, carefully place the fried balls into the syrup. Let them simmer in the syrup for at least 5-6 minutes, allowing the balls to absorb the flavors.

6 Turn off the heat and cover the pan, allowing the Gulab Jamun to soak in the syrup for at least a couple of hours. The longer they soak, the more flavorful they will become.

7 Once the Gulab Jamun has cooled down, they are ready to be served. Optionally, you can garnish them with chopped nuts or saffron strands before serving. Enjoy!

KETO MAHALABIA

Directions

1. In a small bowl, combine 3 tablespoons of almond flour with enough almond milk to mix until well combined.

2. In a non-stick pan, heat the remaining almond milk over medium heat.

3. Gradually add the mixture to the warm milk in the pan. Stir it and add the cream and sweetener. Stir continuously as the mixture thickens.

4. Add the cardamom powder and continue cooking and stirring until it reaches a boiling point and thickens further.

5. Remove from heat and stir in the rosewater.

6. Transfer the mixture to glasses, put in the refrigerator and let chill for at least 3 hours. Before serving, garnish with pistachios and rose petals.

Ingredients

200 ml Almond milk

100 g Cream

3 tbsp Almond flour

3 tbsp Erythritol

1 tsp Rose water

1/2 tsp Cardamom powder

KETO DONUTS

Directions

1 Preheat your oven to 180°C . Generously grease a 12-count donut pan and set it aside.

2 In a mixing bowl, combine the almond flour, sweetener, and baking soda. Mix well.

3 In a separate bowl, whisk together the eggs, apple cider vinegar, and coconut milk.
Add the wet ingredients to the dry ingredients and mix until just combined.

4 Transfer the donut batter into a ziplock bag. Cut one end of the bag and gently squeeze the batter into the donut pan.

5 Bake the donuts for 12-15 minutes.

6 Remove from the oven and let them cool for 5 minutes before transferring to a wire rack to cool completely.

7 If desired, frost the donuts with your favorite frosting.

Ingredients

255 grams almond flour

100 grams granulated sweetener of choice

1 teaspoon baking soda

4 large eggs

1 teaspoon apple cider vinegar

60 ml coconut milk (you can use any milk of choice)

Printed in Great Britain
by Amazon

46695193R00094